RAIDERS
of the
CIVIL WAR

RAIDERS
of the
CIVIL WAR

UNTOLD STORIES OF ACTIONS BEHIND THE LINES

RUSS A. PRITCHARD JR.

THE LYONS PRESS
Guilford, Connecticut
An imprint of The Globe Pequot Press

Credits
Project Manager: Ray Bonds
Designers: Tony Stocks, Compendium Publishing, and Ian Hughes
Cartographer: Michael G. Marino
U.S. Graphic Consultant: Jennifer Houck
Printed and bound in China

Library of Congress Cataloging-in-Publication Data

Pritchard, Russ A.
    Raiders of the Civil War : untold stories of actions behind the lines / Russ A.
Pritchard, Jr.
        p. cm.
    Includes bibliographical references and index.
    ISBN 1-59228-619-4 (trade cloth)
    1. United States—History—Civil War, 1861–1865—Campaigns—Anecdotes.
2. United States—History—Civil War, 1861–1865—Cavalry operations—
Anecdotes. 3. United States—History—Civil War, 1861–1865—Naval
operations—Anecdotes. 4. Raids (Military science)—History—19th century.
5. United States. Army—History—Civil War, 1861–1865—Anecdotes. 6.
Confederate States of America. Army—History—Anecdotes. 7. United States.
Army—Officers—Biography—Anecdotes. 8. Confederate States of America.
Army—Officers—Biography—Anecdotes. I. Title.
E470.P75 2005
973.7'3—dc22
                                                                        2005044143

The Author
Russ A. Pritchard, Jr., is a graduate of The Choate School, Wallingford,
Connecticut, and Washington and Lee University, Lexington, Virginia.
He was Executive Director of the Civil War Library and Museum in
Philadelphia from 1976 until 1995. Mr. Pritchard has written, and acted
as technical advisor to, many books related to the Civil War and other
books of historical interest. He is now retired and lives in Tennessee and
Mississippi.

Acknowledgments
Very many people have been extraordinarily helpful in the preparation of
this volume. The author and publishers wish to thank in particular the
following.

James R. Johnston and the staff of the History Department of the Memphis Shelby County Public Library and Information Center, who generously provided suggestions and illustrations from their holdings. Dave
Dermon, II, provided resources from his personal library, artifacts from
his collection, suggested a photographer, Lee C. Arnoult, and then provided a location for the photo shoot to be done. John Ashworth, Phil
Griffith and Jim Koch provided examples from their collections. Tom
Glass, Dean Thomas and Gary Adelman were instrumental in obtaining
many images. Erin and Christopher Lee, John Montague, Sandy Mc-
Common, and Ed Archer were equally obliging. Paul Calame, and Nora
and Wallace Witmer supplied information that would have been missed.
Carl E. Johnson gave permission to reproduce from his fascinating book-
let on the St. Albans Raid. William A. Penn provided an illustration of
Morgan's raid on Cynthiana, Kentucky, in July 1862. Melinda Day carried out splendid photographic research work on maritime aspects. Bill
Slater and his wife took a lot of trouble sending photographs of the
monument erected in honor of Nathan Bedford Forrest, of which one
was selected (copyright 2004 by William F. Slater, III, Chicago, Illinois,
used by permission). Mark Fowlkes sent a great selection of photos asso-
ciated with his great grandfather, George W. Bowman, of Lebanon,
Kentucky, who was a cavalryman of the 2nd Kentucky Cavalry, Duke's
Regiment, under the command of General John Hunt Morgan. Michael
G. Marino did an excellent job of sorting through references to create
very helpful maps. And Ron Rowe of Newmark USA kindly provided an
image taken from Robert Summers' painting, "Rebel Raiders," for use
on the cover. (Art prints by Robert Summers can be seen on the Internet
at www.newmarkusa.com.)

Robin and Wesley Ashworth were especially accommodating, while Jennifer Houck cheerfully gave extremely helpful technical support.

Mary Ann Weaver Lee repeatedly asked when the project would be finished, but she was always there.

Russ A. Pritchard, Jr.
Collierville, Tennessee

Additional illustrations
Page 1: John Singleton Mosby, probably the most audacious raider of
the war.

Pages 2-3: Primary targets of the South's raiders were the Union's supply
lines, including railroads.

Page 4: George Armstrong Custer typified the daring, cavalier Civil War
raider.

Contents

Introduction

Below: By mid-1863 the Union cavalrymen had learned all the lessons the hard way. Those that survived were tough, seasoned veterans, an even match for the Confederate cavalrymen who were markedly superior during the first two years of the war. The resolute, professional appearance of this cavalryman is typical of the Union riders in the latter part of the conflict.

Students of the American Civil War have debated the strategic effect of raids during the conflict almost since the war ended. A few have adopted the stance that raids were of no real importance, providing little more than momentary annoyance and copy for the press of the time. However, most believe that raids made substantial contributions to the conduct of the war, and this observation seems to have the most merit. The psychological impact alone of raids should not be underestimated; they unquestionably affected the morale of both combatants and citizens of the North and South at various times.

The raider, whether he was Confederate, Federal or out-of-uniform partisan or guerrilla on either side was a special kind of soldier. These individuals had certain qualities that set them apart from more conventional fighting men. That they were all incredibly brave, and

some of them foolhardy, can be taken for granted; but they also possessed those special traits of imagination, self-sufficiency, audacity, and determination. These qualities combined to produce a highly motivated soldier who performed well under independent command or as a member of a small special group under extraordinary and stressful conditions. Such men were able to adapt to and maximize the advantages of the rapid changes in modes of warfare that were occurring during the mid-19th century.

Mounted troops evolved from heavy dragoons armed with saber or lance into highly mobile light cavalry carrying breech-loading or repeating carbines and revolvers. Their mission changed from one of shock troops to that of intelligence gatherers, the eyes and ears of the army, and, at the same time, fast-moving riders capable of delivering precision assaults

Left: Confederate raiders developed railroad destruction to a fine science. This devastation to the Orange & Alexandria Railroad is the result of only a few hours' work, just a scant thirty-five miles away from Washington City. These will-o-the-wisp riders destroyed Northern rail systems and telegraph communications almost at will early in the war, but this changed as Federal rear-area maintenance units like this became more organized. By the end of the conflict, Federal repair crews had developed their skills to such a high degree that they often managed to minimize rail traffic disruption.

at selected targets. Horses became a mode of transportation as the men more often fought on foot after arriving on the battlefield, depending upon the advantage of the firepower of their advanced weapons to win the day.

Other rapidly developing technology was a major factor during the war. Railroads became very important as the military implications of their use in supply and communication became readily apparent to both sides, a fact recognized by European strategists as early as 1836. The North had over 22,000 miles of track at the start of the war. The South had less than 9,000 miles of track, a considerable amount of it in the immediate theater of the war and vulnerable to attack. Thus, railroads became strategic targets for raids, with the disruption of supply and communications being a primary aim. Not only were locomotives and rolling stock considered targets but also the rails themselves and bridges on which they were laid.

The North, as a result of the Railways and Telegraph Act of January 31, 1862, organized

Left: The fine trestle of the Richmond, Fredericksburg & Potomac Railroad over Potomac Creek was a prime target and was destroyed by Confederates. It was replaced by this 400-foot-long tottering marvel of engineering built in just nine days in May 1862, using more than two million feet of lumber cut at the site. The common soldiers that built the structure had no specialized tools and didn't even remove the bark from the timbers. President Lincoln commented that it was nothing more than beanpoles and cornstalks.

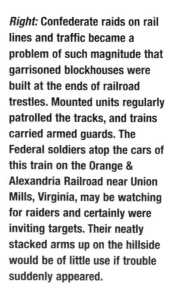

Above: Raids during the Civil War had specific primary targets. Railroads and communications were always first and foremost. Depriving the enemy of his source of supplies and the ability to communicate with subordinate commands made him ineffectual. Release of prisoners of war to recover manpower and free them from hardship imposed by the enemy had great propaganda appeal. This image illustrates two such targets: Confederate prisoners awaiting transport to Northern prisons, and the huge rail yards at Chattanooga.

Right: Confederate raids on rail lines and traffic became a problem of such magnitude that garrisoned blockhouses were built at the ends of railroad trestles. Mounted units regularly patrolled the tracks, and trains carried armed guards. The Federal soldiers atop the cars of this train on the Orange & Alexandria Railroad near Union Mills, Virginia, may be watching for raiders and certainly were inviting targets. Their neatly stacked arms up on the hillside would be of little use if trouble suddenly appeared.

its lines and also developed the United States Military Railroad. Northern industry insured replacement stock for that which was damaged by Confederate forces. But the South had little replacement capability for track and equipment, a constant target, once destroyed. The Confederacy was never able to organize its railroad lines to their full advantage. By 1865, the Southern railway system had collapsed, and this was a major factor in the Confederate defeat.

Military minds quickly recognized the advantage of telegraph communication and both

sides used code and ciphers because each tapped the other's line. The U.S. Military Telegraph Service was established and eventually utilized some 6,400 miles of wire, some of it underwater. Confederate forces also used the telegraph but their system was much smaller and never approached the efficiency of their counterpart. These wires, miles of which conveniently paralleled railroads, became natural targets of opportunity for raiders.

Quartermaster installations, supply depots, remount stations, ordnance storage facilities and rail yards provided more conventional targets for fast-moving raiders. Confederate forces were always plagued by shortages of every kind, so special attention was given to this type of target as a ready means to refit and re-supply units in need of arms, clothing, food and equipment. It was no idle jest when someone said that the Federal Ordnance and Quartermaster Departments were the best in the world; they supplied two armies, both the Federal and Confederate, for the four years of the war.

Naturally, manpower losses were a major concern to both forces but much more critical to the South. For this reason prisoner-of-war installations were of special interest. At one time or another Confederate and Federal forces entertained plans for massive prisoner snatches from various camps. A number of these fanciful

ideas came close to reality but, in hindsight, even substantial numbers of released prisoners deep behind enemy lines, at various levels of poor health and with no equipment, would not have been a particularly dangerous adversary. The idea sounded much better than the actuality, but fear of such an event forced both sides to allocate units to guard against such an eventuality. Just this defensive utilization of military assets was in many cases the objective of raiders and a victory in itself.

Time after time a smaller, inferior force preying on the fears of the civilian population forced the enemy's military to utilize a much larger number of troops just to guard rear areas, depriving the army of their presence in the combat theater. This was the beauty of the raider, the partisan and the guerrilla. A small active group could effectively tie down an enormously superior number of troops by their presence alone.

Raids were also effective in the rivers and on the sea. The North had the advantage of a large maritime fleet and an existing navy, albeit a small one, and almost immediately declared a blockade. The South, with little afloat, had ingenuity, a number of intrepid sailors and some 3,500 miles of coast. The Confederacy realized from the start that its nonexistent navy could not fight the Union navy ship for ship, but it could attack its defenseless maritime fleet and inflict enormous economic damage, and that was the course it chose.

Individuals on both sides developed ingenious special units and tactics for audacious riverine assaults on a variety of targets. The names of many of these men, such as George Custer, J. E. B. Stuart, Raphael Semmes, Phil Sheridan, Nathan Bedford Forrest, and Wade Hampton are well known; others, such as Earl Van Dorn, Benjamin Grierson, Judson Kilpatrick and Jubal Early, less so, but few remember Lieutenant Bennett Young or James J. Andrews. Others are so infamous, such as the guerrilla Quantrill, as to be unforgettable, yet some are so obscure that they are almost unknown, like John Yates Beall. Recent events such as the raising of the Confederate submarine CSS *Hunley* have brought recognition to the names of Horace Hunley and Lieutenant

Below: **The U.S. steamer *Harriet Lane* was the side-wheel ship that resupplied Fort Sumter and fired the first shot of the Civil War. She served in North Carolina and was at the engagements at Forts Jackson and St. Phillip in the lower Mississippi. In winter 1862 the steamer was part of the Federal fleet that captured Galveston and became part of the West Gulf Blockade Squadron. Confederate Major General John B. Magruder developed a surprise combined naval and land attack on the town and the Union fleet, executed on January 1, 1863. The operation was incredibly successful. *Harriet Lane* was captured and became the blockade-runner *Lavinia*, while the Federal flagship *Westfield* was burned to prevent capture. The audacious assault raised the blockade of Galveston for a time.**

Right: Major General Thomas Jonathan "Stonewall" Jackson was a strong proponent of unconventional warfare. He was a risk taker who often divided his command in the face of superior numbers so as to steal a march and strike an unsuspecting adversary on an exposed flank. His eccentric ability to think outside the conventional military box of the times and discover enemy weak points made him a very dangerous opponent. Many a Federal commander was bested by Jackson's tendency to do the unexpected and his ability to appear out of nowhere.

George Dixon. All of these men and the events in which they were major participants form one of the most exciting aspects of the American Civil War that continues to fascinate generation after generation.

It is evident that unconventional warfare had a far greater impact on the conduct of the war than numbers would suggest. Cavalry, already obsolescent as a heavy shock element, reinvented itself as a highly mobile reconnaissance and strike force and extended its military usefulness into the 20th century. The development of what we know today as surgical strikes and special weapons and tactics began to emerge. The psychological impact on the civilian population required withdrawal of large numbers of troops from combat to cope with infinitely smaller numbers of elusive raiders, and greatly affected military tactics and strategy.

Some people have said raiders and raids were no more than a diversion, a little sideshow of the big show. To the contrary, it appears that many raids did affect the war, maybe not the outcome, but certainly the way it was fought. The delay incurred by Grant in the Vicksburg Campaign caused by Van Dorn's raid on Holly Springs is just one example. The disastrous destruction of the commercial and whaling fleets by Confederate high seas raiders resulted in economic repercussions into the 20th century. Also, raids produced some of the great "what ifs" of the war. Just suppose Jubal Early had captured Washington and President Lincoln....

General Robert E. Lee said in April 1865, "A partisan war may be continued, and hostilities protracted, causing individual suffering and the devastation of the country. To save useless effusion of blood, I would recommend measures be taken for suspension of hostilities and the restoration of peace." The wisdom of General Lee spared the country from a vicious and pointless guerrilla war that could have carried on for years and engendered bitterness that would have lasted for decades. Lee's recommendation brought peace to the defeated and demoralized South. With the conventional end to the conflict, without wholesale imprisonment or execution of the vanquished, the country began to rebuild and reunite, something that makes this nation unique in the history of civil wars.

However, to go back to the beginning, it is no small coincidence that the prelude to this war, so influenced by raiders, was in fact a raid conducted some sixteen months prior to the outbreak of hostilities, led by a fanatical psychopath named John Brown.

John Brown's Raid: October 16-18, 1859

Brown was born in 1800, in West Torrington, Connecticut, into a dysfunctional family. He married twice and fathered twenty children, moved about frequently, was involved in multiple lawsuits and failed miserably in no fewer than fifteen business endeavors. At some point, he admitted there was a strong strain of insanity in his family. As an adult he embraced the cause of abolition with singular devotion. In pursuit of this obsession he became notorious as a murderer and terrorist. He believed he was God's chosen instrument to rid the country of slavery. The outrageous belief that he murdered in the name of the Lord actually won him surprising support among the more radical abolitionist groups in the North, and there is no doubt he was a very charismatic orator.

In 1855 Brown and five of his sons appeared in Kansas territory to fan the flames of animosity that already existed between pro-slavery and "free-soiler" factions in the area. In mid-May pro-slavery forces raided and sacked the town of Lawrence, the center of abolitionist sentiment in the state. The raid infuriated Brown and he retaliated. On the night of May 24, 1856, Brown and some of his family committed ritual murder along Potawatomi Creek, hacking to death with swords five unarmed pro-slavery citizens. The corpses of James Doyle, his two teenage sons, William and Drury, neighbors Allen Wilkenson and William Sherman were dismembered and otherwise abused. The abolitionist press somehow managed to view the Potawatomi Massacre as a noble act and Brown became a hero in Boston, but in Kansas he was already a terrorist.

Brown appeared in the Harpers Ferry, Virginia, area in early July 1859 using the assumed name of Isaac Smith. He rented the small Kennedy farm near Sharpsburg, Maryland. Brown's plan was to capture the U.S. arsenal at Harpers Ferry and use the weapons there to arm a slave rebellion in the South. His disciples gradually assembled and large crates of Sharps carbines, pikes and revolvers arrived. The raiders planned their attack carefully, with specific tasks assigned to different assault teams. Incredibly, however, Brown did not consider any kind of contingency plan or line of retreat should withdrawal become necessary. He irrationally expected a spontaneous massive slave uprising.

At 8:00 PM on Sunday, October 16, the group of abolitionists, twenty-two men in total, five black and seventeen white, each of them armed with a Sharps carbine and two revolvers, launched the raid. Brown drove a one-horse wagon hauling tools, ammunition and some of the pikes. Eighteen men of the assault force (Brown's sons Oliver and Watson, John Kagi, John Edwin Cook, Aaron D. Stevens, Dauphin Thompson, Dangerfield Newby, Edwin Coppoc, William Thompson, William Henry Leeman, Steward Taylor, Osbome Perry Anderson, John A. Copeland, Lewis Sherrard Leary, Sheilds Green, Albert Hazlett, Jerry Anderson, and Charles Plummer Tidd) followed noiselessly on foot through the moonless night toward the undefended arsenal. Three of the group, Owen Brown, Barclay Coppoc and Francis J. Merriam, remained behind at the farm to guard supplies and arm slaves who were expected to rally to the cause.

The raiders quietly deployed across the Baltimore & Ohio Railroad bridge into Virginia around 11:00 PM, capturing all watchmen at various locations with no difficulty. Cook and Tidd cut the

Left: John Brown, terrorist, murderer and martyr. His actions served to polarize simmering feelings in the North and South and became a galvanizing catalyst to events that resulted in four years of bloody Civil War. Brown's sincerity and beliefs have never been doubted, notwithstanding his repugnant tactics.

telegraph wires. Watson Brown and Taylor were left to hold the bridge over the Potomac. Oliver Brown and William Thompson held the bridge over the Shenandoah. Other elements took possession of the armory and the arsenal while Kagi and Copeland seized Hall's Rifle Works. Stevens and Cook took a detail out to the plantation of Lewis W. Washington, a man of local prominence and great-grand-nephew of the first president, seized him and other hostages and armed several of his slaves with pikes. In just a few hours all the Federal property and several million dollars' worth of arms were under Brown's control. Not a shot had been fired.

The eastbound night express train from Wheeling to Baltimore arrived about 1:00 AM Monday. The train stopped at Wager House, a station just before the bridge, and was about to proceed when Patrick Higgins, one of the captured watchmen who had just escaped from the raiders, ran up and warned Phelps, the conductor, that the bridge was blocked and something was amiss. Just then Heyward Shepherd, a black porter, came up from the

rear of the train to investigate. Brown's men started shooting and mortally wounded Shepherd, ironically a free black man. He was carried into Wager House where he soon died, the first casualty of the raid.

By this time, the shooting, the commotion in the streets as the raiders seized installations, and the noise of the standing train alerted the sleeping townsfolk that something unusual was happening. Thomas Boerley, a local grocer, innocently walked into one of the assault groups and was shot down, the first white man killed, and the second casualty. For some inexplicable reason, at dawn, around 5:00 AM, the raiders allowed the train to go on and when the train crew arrived in Monocacy and then Frederick, they alerted the whole country.

In the meantime, as citizens appeared on the streets of Harpers Ferry they were taken hostage by Brown's men. Soon, the Lutheran Church bell started clanging wildly and a local doctor who attended the dying Shepherd across the river mounted his horse and rode to Charlestown, Virginia, after first dispatching another rider to Shepherdstown, spreading

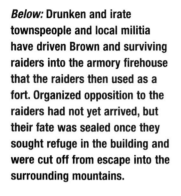

Below: Drunken and irate townspeople and local militia have driven Brown and surviving raiders into the armory firehouse that the raiders then used as a fort. Organized opposition to the raiders had not yet arrived, but their fate was sealed once they sought refuge in the building and were cut off from escape into the surrounding mountains.

word of the incident. By mid-morning groups of drunken and armed townsmen had assembled and began isolated firefights with several raider groups. Soon the first militia units from the neighborhood arrived. The Jefferson Guards, without uniforms and armed with shotguns and squirrel rifles, took the Potomac Bridge around noon, and the Charlestown Guards regained control of the Shenandoah Bridge.

The first raider killed was Dangerfield Newby, a black man. The irate townspeople cut off his ears and threw his body in the gutter. The citizens were out of control, militia units had no coordinated chain of command, and the situation was rapidly becoming a vigilante action. Subsequently, Brown's dwindling party was forced to take cover in the engine house, a brick building used to house horse-drawn pumpers and hose trucks near the gate of the arsenal complex.

In the early afternoon, realizing that his raiders could not escape, Brown tried to negotiate. The first emissary he sent out was seized and taken captive to the Galt House and sub-sequently killed. Brown then sent his son, Watson, and another man out under a flag of truce. Both were shot down by the enraged townspeople, but Watson managed to drag himself back inside the engine house mortally wounded. Another of Brown's men was killed on a bridge trying to escape, and his body used for target practice and the amusement of the mob.

Kagi and his cohorts were driven out of the rifle works and one was killed, another mortally wounded. A third was captured and was about to be lynched but was saved for a time by a kindly doctor. Shortly thereafter, around 4:00 PM, the town mayor, Fontaine Beckham, was killed and the frenzied mob seized and killed the captured raider, his corpse being used for target practice. The three men back at the farm realized all was lost and melted away. Night fell and the Brown party, huddled in the freezing cold of the engine house, began to realize that surrender might no longer be an option.

Meanwhile, the government in Washington was momentarily stunned, but then reacted.

Below: Marines from Washington under the overall command of U.S. Army Colonel Robert E. Lee and Marine Lieutenant Israel Green use a stout ladder as a battering ram to bash in one of the thick doors of the firehouse, in preparation for the assault on the raiders and rescue of hostages trapped in the small building.

President Buchanan at first was told several hundred white and black insurrectionists held the arsenal and this report was multiplied tenfold by rumor and hysteria. The telegraph across the country began to carry wild stories of a Negro insurrection at Harpers Ferry.

The whole police force of the capital was called out, with patrolmen stationed on every road. Militia units all over Maryland and Virginia were called up. By 1:30 PM the president ordered Brevet Colonel Robert E. Lee, Lieutenant J. E. B. Stuart and some ninety marines from Washington Barracks to proceed immediately to Harpers Ferry where Lee would take command.

Lee and Stuart arrived from Washington around midnight Monday and Lee brought order to chaos. The marines under Lieutenant Israel Green and the various militia units surrounded the engine house and waited for dawn. At 5:00 AM the marines and militia were ready to move in on the raiders. All spectators had been cleared from the area.

The engine house was a brick structure measuring about 35 by 30 feet. Inside, Brown's defensive position was a strong one. The only entrance was through three strong, ironbound, heavy wood double doors in the front of the structure. Lee ordered Stuart to approach the building, present a note demanding Brown's immediate surrender, but under no

circumstances to allow negotiations. If surrender was not immediate, Stuart was to wave his hat as a signal for the marine assault party under Lieutenant Green to attack the building.

The marines were drawn up in the arsenal yard. Stuart walked to the right-hand door and handed the note to Brown, who read it and began to tell Stuart his demands. Stuart jumped aside and waved his hat, and the marines charged the door. Sledgehammers failed to open the door so it was battered in with a heavy ladder. Two marines were killed during the breech and two of Brown's men were bayoneted during the melee.

Lieutenant Green, one of the first to enter, saw Colonel Washington, one of the hostages. The colonel pointed to Brown, whom Green attacked with his sword. His first thrust was deflected by Brown's belt buckle. Green closed with his adversary and clubbed him on the head with his sword hilt, eventually knocking him to the floor The whole assault took only two or three minutes. Brown and four others survived but ten raiders lay dead or dying and the others had run for the hills.

Brown was jailed, tried and found guilty of the crimes of treason, insurrection and murder. While awaiting execution he apparently warned his captors: "You may dispose of me very easily – but this question has still to be

Right: Painting illustrating the release of the hostages and removal of the dead and wounded from the firehouse. John Brown was carried out after his confrontation with Lieutenant Green and is shown laying in the right foreground under guard of four marines in greatcoats. Lee, Stuart and Green are depicted standing at the far right.

settled, the Negro question I mean." The fanatical abolitionist was hanged at Charlestown on December 2, 1859, under strict security provided in part by Major Thomas Jonathan Jackson and the cadets of the Virginia Military Institute. In the large crowd was the popular actor, John Wilkes Booth (who on April 14, 1865, assassinated President Abraham Lincoln).

Contrary to heroic depictions of Brown's execution, he had no eloquent last words. James W. Campbell, sheriff, and John Avis, deputy sheriff, who escorted him to the gallows, said he was neither cowardly nor brave. The often seen illustration of Brown kissing a Negro child in his mother's arms was an absolute fabrication. Brown's only words were about the beautiful countryside and the weather and, on the gallows, he said only, "Be quick."

The ever-strident Northern press transformed the bloodthirsty terrorist into a martyred saint almost overnight, and he became the symbol of the abolitionist cause. His body was eventually buried near the family farm in North Elba, Connecticut, surrounded by the Adirondack Mountains.

The song known as The Battle Hymn of the Republic became popular after the beginning of hostilities. The melody is attributed to South Carolinian William Steffe about 1856. The words came several years later:

John Brown's body lies a-moldering in the grave,
John Brown's body lies a-moldering in the grave,
But his truth goes marching on.
Glory, glory hallelujah, etc.

They are attributed to a choral group of the 2nd Massachusetts Infantry. The first formal presentation of the song by the group occurred March 1, 1862, at Charlestown, at the site of Brown's execution. The tune with the words became a very popular song with Federal troops throughout the war and it has become familiar to most people today.

The engine house, John Brown's Fort, was the only Harpers Ferry armory building that survived the war. In 1893 the structure was moved to Chicago for the Columbian Exposition as a tourist attraction. This effort was a dismal failure and the building was abandoned in a vacant lot. It was rescued in 1895, returned to Harpers Ferry and moved several times. Harpers Ferry was declared a national monument in 1944 and a national park in 1963. The National Park Service acquired the structure in 1960 and erected it in the restored district of the town in 1968, about 150 feet east of the original location that is now covered by a railroad right of way.

Brown was immortalized by Stephen Vincent Benet's Pulitzer Prize–winning poem, "John Brown's Body," published in 1928. Subsequently, the poem has been read in countless venues, performed on the stage as a play and even as a musical on Broadway. The raid on Harpers Ferry has been the subject of two motion pictures, *Santa Fe Trail* in 1940 and *God's Angry Man*, also titled *Seven Angry Men*, in 1955. Actor Raymond Massey portrayed John Brown in both films and was nominated for an Oscar in the earlier film. Errol Flynn portrayed J. E. B. Stuart, and Ronald Reagan played George Custer in the first epic.

Brown was praised by liberal minds of the time but others called him a murderer and terrorist. There are no memorials, parks, statues or postage stamps commemorating John Brown. Unquestionably, he was a harbinger of the Civil War and his raid brought the specter of terror to both North and South.

Left: Colonel Robert E. Lee of the U.S. Army had overall command of the military forces at Harpers Ferry in 1859. One of his subordinates was J. E. B. Stuart, then a lieutenant in the regular army. These two Federal officers played a primary role in the capture of John Brown, leader of the first raid and harbinger of the Civil War soon to come.

RAIDS ON
LAND

The raid was a sudden attack by a selected force on part of the enemy's territory or armed forces with a specific mission to obtain or destroy resources, gain information, or disrupt lines of communication. The key to a successful raid was meticulous planning, followed by more planning, followed by review and re-evaluation right up until the raid was launched. Flexibility and adaptability during the execution phase were necessary. Successful raids ended with planned withdrawals, a major shortcoming of John Brown's prewar failed effort.

Raids were often employed by an inferior adversary to harass a superior foe and made maximum use of surprise and deception to even the odds. This was particularly true of Confederate efforts throughout the war. An agile, mounted force was the ideal instrument and cavalry was almost always the branch of service of choice. It is no surprise that the first land raid was executed by Lieutenant Colonel Nathan Bedford Forrest's cavalry riding into Federal-held territory in Kentucky in November 1861. It is also no coincidence that when the old horse cavalry was replaced by armored fighting vehicles in the mid-20th century, some of the tanks were named after those bold leaders. The light Stuart tank and the medium Sherman tank obviously trace their roots to raiders of the Civil War.

The Northern and Southern newspapers both trumpeted accounts of the feats of swashbuckling Confederate raider John Singleton Mosby, to the chagrin of Federal authorities. Typically exaggerated news stories attributed almost mythic abilities to Mosby and his men. This illustration from the September 5, 1863, issue of *Harper's Weekly* depicts yet another raid by the fearless Mosby's guerrillas on a hapless Federal supply train.

The Great Locomotive Chase

One of the most famous raids of the Civil War was the Andrews Raid, popularly known as "The Great Locomotive Chase." The original plan sprang from the fertile mind of James J. Andrews, a mysterious Federal spy. He had already made one unsuccessful attempt to steal a train, but the idea still seemed viable to him.

Andrews and General O. M. Mitchel planned the mission as concomitant actions. Mitchel would attack Huntsville, Alabama, distracting Confederate forces in northern Alabama and Georgia, while Andrews with a small raiding party would simultaneously destroy the Western & Atlantic Railroad, the major supply line from Atlanta to Chattanooga, isolating the garrison there. Andrews would confirm the success of his mission, whereupon Mitchel would move on Chattanooga. The date chosen for the joint operation was April 11, 1862.

Andrews' party numbered twenty-two men, mostly volunteers from the Army of the Ohio, some with civilian railroading experience, including engineers W. W. Brown and W. J. Knight. Andrews gathered his group together near Shelbyville, Tennessee, on the evening of April 7. He made the dangers crystal clear to his men, and told them they would operate behind enemy lines, out of uniform, and were liable to be hanged as spies. Andrews armed the men with revolvers and instructed them to rendezvous at Marietta, Georgia, by midnight April 10. It then began to rain and it never stopped for ten days.

The raiders infiltrated over a hundred miles in three days. Andrews assumed General Mitchel's assault on Huntsville would be delayed by the weather and postponed his part of the mission for twenty-four hours. This was his first mistake, because Mitchel took Huntsville on schedule.

The great adventure began Saturday morning, April 12, in Atlanta, when the *The General,* a 4-4-0-type wood-burning engine built by Rogers, Ketchum and Grosvenor in 1855, pulled a mixed train out of the station at 4:00 AM on the regular 12-hour run to Chattanooga, some 138 miles to the north. The raiders boarded an hour later at Marietta.

Andrews seized the train at Big Shanty because there was no telegraph office there, and it

was the regular breakfast stop for crew and passengers. Camp McDonald, a Confederate training camp, was adjacent to the tracks but posed little threat. The raiders observed that the Southern troops were armed mostly with pikes, few of them were in uniform, and some were barefoot – not a particularly fearsome foe.

The train crew and passengers went to the Lacy House to eat at about 6:00 AM. As they walked, Andrews and his men loitered in the rear, and then Andrews, Knight, and two others climbed quickly into the cab of *The General* while the other men spread over the train. Several of the raiders uncoupled the passenger cars and climbed aboard the empty boxcars. In the cab, Andrews ordered the throttle opened as the train accelerated out of the station to the screech of spinning wheels on rails.

William Allen Fuller, the 26 year old conductor, and Jeff Cain, the engineer, happened to look out of the window of the hotel in time to see the train disappearing down the tracks. Fuller was personally stung by the loss of his train. It was a blot on his honor. Fuller and Cain bolted out of the hotel and were joined by Anthony Murphy, a Western & Atlantic shop foreman, and the three men sprinted on foot after the disappearing train.

Andrews and his men cut the telegraph wire near Moon Station and picked up a pry bar from some workers. The raiders maintained normal speed through Acworth and Allatoona so as to avoid unwanted attention, and cut the telegraph wire after each station. They also picked up some loose railroad ties and placed them in a boxcar. Andrews removed a rail from the track past Allatoona and they took that with them too.

The Yankees, unaware of any pursuit and with the wires cut and track disabled behind them, crossed the long bridge over the Etowah River, where they saw the engine *Yonah* on a branch line. The engineer implored Andrews to burn the bridge and destroy the engine but Andrews, perhaps over-confident at this point, didn't want to cause alarm and continued north. This decision became his second mistake.

Fuller ran the two miles to Moon's Station where he found a handcar, and with Cain and Murphy continued the chase, pumping frantically, to catch the train. At Acworth they

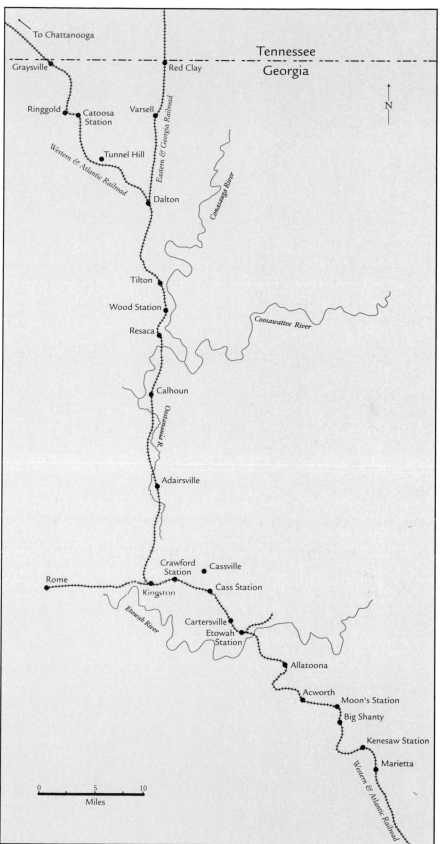

Above: Route of the Great Locomotive Chase on the Atlantic & Western Railroad.

Illustration by Michael G. Marino

Right: Confederates in Pursuit, an illustration by Isaac Walton Taber, a prolific artist and illustrator for *The Century Magazine*. The action shows the Confederates, then aboard *Yonah* that Fuller had commandeered at Etowah, flying toward the blocked rail yard at Kingston.

learned that the wire was cut and it was then that they suddenly realized the train had been stolen by Union raiders! In their haste they didn't see the missing rail, and their handcar careened into a ditch. No one was hurt, and the wheezing men manhandled the car back on the tracks and continued pursuit. Arriving at Etowah, they spied the *Yonah* and quickly had the old engine flying after *The General*.

As Fuller and crew aboard *Yonah* closed the gap, the raiders lost over an hour tensely waiting for three oncoming trains to clear the

Above: Track and station on the Western & Atlantic Railroad at Allatoona Pass. Andrews and his men stopped here to cut telegraph wires and pile railroad ties on the track in a futile effort to stop Confederate pursuers. The raiders removed track four miles north of here and thought they were home free, but they didn't know William Fuller.

Right: The restored *Texas*, also a Western & Atlantic Engine, that William Fuller and the persistent Confederates used to chase *The General* for much of the pursuit, now part of the exhibit at the Atlanta Cyclorama and Civil War Museum.

of the Southern railroaders in pursuit, removed another rail north of Kingston.

The Confederates covered the fourteen miles to Kingston in fifteen minutes and found the Kingston yard blocked. Fuller left *Yonah*, ran through the yard and seized the engine *Wm. R. Smith* from a passenger train on the Rome line. Here he learned that *The General* was just four minutes ahead. Now, alert to missing rails, Fuller perched on the cow-catcher on the front of the *Wm. R. Smith* to see the tracks ahead as the Confederates chased after their fleeing engine.

Soon, for the first time, Andrews and his men heard the whistle of Fuller's engine and realized they were in trouble. They tried to remove another section of rail but failed and continued in their flight north, steaming through Calhoun, barely avoiding a head-on collision with a southbound train.

Just in time, Fuller and companions spied the missing rail north of Kingston, and stopped the engine. Cain was exhausted and could not continue, but undaunted, Fuller and

bottleneck at Kingston yards. Andrews persuaded the increasingly curious Confederates that his train was a special unit rushing ammunition to General Beauregard, and sped on his way. Andrews and his men, still unaware

Left: Painting by Wilbur G. Kurtz, 1882-1967, *Texas at the Tunnel.* Kurtz produced a series of paintings chronicling the chase and aftermath. He was well qualified, having married William Fuller's daughter, Annie Laurie, in 1911. Kurtz was the technical consultant for the movies *Gone With the Wind*, 1939, *Song of the South*, 1946, and *The Great Locomotive Chase*, 1957.

Below: Tracks of the Western & Atlantic Railroad leading into the long tunnel at Tunnel Hill. Smoke from *The General* was still pouring out of the tunnel when Fuller on *Texas* approached and, fearing an ambush, slowed his pursuit. Andrews and his men outgunned the Confederates and should have stood and fought at this point. Andrews' decision to continue the race sealed their doom.

Murphy continued the chase for three miles, on foot again. Two miles below Adairsville they met a freight train pulled by the engine *Texas*, a Danforth, Cooke & Company eight-wheeler, with engineer Peter Bracken, fireman Henry Haney and wood-passer Alonzo Martin. Cars were dumped on a siding at Adairsville and the *Texas*, in reverse, took off after *The General*. Fuller stopped at Calhoun Station and picked up Captain W. J. Whitsitt and ten men of the 1st Georgia Volunteers and, shortly thereafter, Dalton telegrapher Edward Henderson, who was searching for a break in the wire cut by the raiders.

The Federals tried to roll one of the boxcars back into the oncoming *Texas*, but the Confederates just pushed it on ahead of them. At the long covered Oostanuala Bridge near Resaca, Andrews tried to set fire to a second car inside the bridge, but because it had been raining so long nothing would burn. The onrushing Confederates just picked up the smoldering car and pushed it on ahead to a siding. Finally, the

raiders broke out the back of the last remaining boxcar and resorted to throwing out ties in the hope of derailing the onrushing *Texas*.

The two engines raced through the hills of northwest Georgia, bringing the raiders ever closer to their objective. The raiders had no time or proper tools to tear up track as planned, or to disrupt pursuit, because Fuller and his dogged band were so close. Heavy rain precluded burning water-soaked bridges. Andrews ordered the engineer to disregard the danger of southbound trains and let *The General* run wide open. The long tunnel at Tunnel Hill provided one last chance for the Federals to ambush the Confederate train. Andrews and his men were better armed and they outnumbered the Southerners, but Andrews decided against it, a fatal and final mistake.

The chase ended just past Ringgold, Georgia, eighteen miles south of Chattanooga, where the engine ran out of steam. The wild ride had covered fifty-one miles. Unbeknown to the Union raiders, General Mitchel had not taken Chattanooga.

Andrews yelled to his intrepid band that it was every man for himself, and they scattered into the surrounding woods. All twenty-two of the raiders were soon captured, however. Andrews was taken to Atlanta, tried, and hanged as a spy at the corner of 3rd and Juniper streets on June 7, 1862. Seven other raiders were hanged on June 18, and all were buried in unmarked graves. The surviving fourteen men escaped in October and eight of them managed to return to Federal lines; the other six were recaptured, but were exchanged in March 1863.

President Abraham Lincoln authorized the Army Medal of Honor on July 14, 1862. Six of the surviving Andrews raiders were the first recipients of the medal on March 25, 1863. Five more of the raiders were awarded the medal posthumously. As a civilian, Andrews was not eligible. After the war, the remains of the executed raiders were reburied in the National Cemetery at Chattanooga.

This fascinating story was not over. The *Texas* remained in service for years. In 1893, the Cyclorama opened in Grant Park in Atlanta and the locomotive was placed on exhibit. Today, the *Texas* is a featured attraction at the Atlanta Cyclorama and Civil War

Museum. *The General* was badly damaged during the Confederate evacuation of Atlanta but was rebuilt in 1868 and ran until retired in 1886. The old engine was an honored attraction at the 1888 Reunion of the Grand Army of the Republic (GAR), the Union veterans' organization, but was then sent to the scrap yard at Vining's Station, Georgia. It was miraculously saved in 1891, restored and placed on exhibit at Union Station in Chattanooga. The venerable engine appeared at major exhibitions around the country, including the 1893 Columbian Exposition in Chicago that featured John Brown's Fort, until 1948. *The General* was restored again in 1961 and moved back to Big Shanty (renamed Kennesaw), as part of the Kennesaw Civil War Museum. Presently, the grand old engine is the centerpiece of The Southern Museum of Civil War and Locomotive History which opened in 2003.

The two engines have become icons of the war. The raid has been the subject of at least two motion pictures and countless stories and articles. The original engine was featured in the classic 1926 silent film, *The General*, starring Buster Keaton, and reached a speed of 55 miles per hour during the chase scenes. Disney Studios made *The Great Locomotive Chase* in color in 1956, with Fess Parker as James J. Andrews and Jeffrey Hunter in the role of the relentless Fuller. The incident will always be one of the most exciting stories of the war.

Above: The General was a popular Civil War attraction at the August 1888 Grand Army of the Republic reunion at Columbus, Ohio. Ten of the eleven surviving members of Andrews' raiders and Captain Fuller gather around the patriotically decorated engine. The photograph was made by Wilbur Kurtz.

Far left above: The Andrews Raid: Clearing the Track, another illustration by Isaac Walton Taber, depicting *Texas*, pursuing in reverse, pushing a burning boxcar dropped by Andrews in the covered bridge over the Oostanaula River, in a futile effort to burn the drenched bridge and stop the tenacious Confederates.

Far left below: The General was used by the Confederates until lost during the evacuation of Atlanta, but it survived the war to be rebuilt in the Western & Atlantic shops and kept in service until 1886. The old engine came very close to being scrapped as she sat at Vining's Station, but was restored yet again in the Nashville, Chattanooga & St. Louis shops in Nashville in 1891.

Streight's Mule Brigade

Below left: Colonel Abel D. Streight, commander of the ill-fated Mule Brigade. While his entourage had its comical aspects, the raid made authorities in northern Alabama realize how vulnerable the area was to Union depredations. After his capture Colonel Streight led one of the great prison escapes of the war from Libby Prison in Richmond.

Below right: General Nathan Bedford Forrest, a legend in his lifetime and whose reputation has only grown with the passage of years. He was wounded in combat several times, had twenty-nine horses killed under him and was said to have killed thirty Federal soldiers in personal combat. Not a man to trifle with.

In late 1862, General Ulysses S. Grant devised a plan for the capture of Vicksburg that would open up the Mississippi River and split the Confederacy in two. As part of this campaign Grant envisioned several diversionary operations to distract forces of General Pemberton, Confederate commander in Mississippi. Colonel Abel D. Streight was chosen to lead one of these diversions. His objective was to cross the state of Alabama and cut the Western & Atlantic Railroad in north Georgia between Atlanta and Chattanooga, severing General Braxton Bragg's supply lines, and forcing him to pull his army out of middle Tennessee. Colonel Benjamin Grierson's raid from LaGrange, Tennessee, was also part of the grand plan.

Streight's raid was an operation where everything that could go wrong did go wrong, a disaster from beginning to end.

Colonel Streight commanded a provisional brigade with an initial strength of 2,000 men, made up of four infantry regiments, the 80th Illinois, 51st Indiana, 73rd Indiana and 3rd Ohio, augmented by two companies of the 1st Middle Tennessee (Union) Cavalry, and a section of the 6th Ohio Light Artillery. Some genius, a rear echelon staff officer, decided that the brigade should be mounted because of the distance to be traveled, and it was thought mules could better traverse the rough terrain in north Alabama. Thus, Streight's "Mule Brigade" was born. The fact that infantrymen were not familiar with the care and riding of mules was ignored. The four regiments involved suddenly became mounted infantry and embarked on a raid deep into Confederate-controlled territory.

The composite group partially outfitted at Nashville and on April 10 embarked on steamers for Palmyra. After arrival they learned that their new mounts were poor, wild, young unbroken mules, some fifty of them already sick with distemper. Other mounts impressed locally were mostly unshod. Streight's men spent a day and a half trying to saddle and break the unmanageable mules, a number of which died.

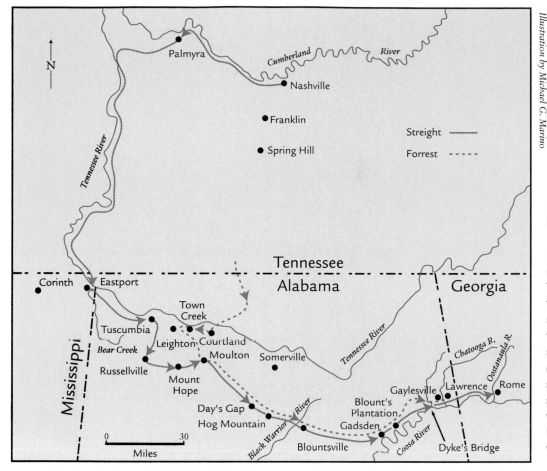

Illustration by Michael G. Marino

Left: Line of march of Streight's Mule Brigade.

Below: An English-made 10-gauge double barrel shotgun. The barrels have been shortened to facilitate mounted use, and a staple and ring have been added to the left lock to enable the shotgun to be suspended from a carbine sling. General Forrest stated, "…the double barrel shotgun is the best gun with which cavalry can be armed." Many of his men carried similar weapons.

Bottom: Brown buff-leather carbine sling with brass Buckle and spring-loaded hook to attach to a ring on the weapon. This piece of equipment provided the rider a convenient method of carrying the arm when on the march and prevented accidental loss during combat.

Already frazzled, the soldiers made a cross-country march and boarded steamers on the Tennessee River to Eastport, Mississippi. Repeated delays culminated eventually in Streight's tardy rendezvous near Eastport with Brigadier General Grenville Dodge, whose force was intended to screen Streight's raiding party. The Dodge-Streight expedition finally began the march to Tuscumbia at 8:00 AM on April 22, several days behind schedule.

At Tuscumbia, Streight sent his sick and lame soldiers back to Corinth, reducing his party to about 1,500 effectives, many of whom were still dismounted. The two forces separated.

Right: Counter-assault of dismounted troopers of the 3rd Ohio and 80th Illinois against Forrest's artillery at Sand Mountain, April 30, 1863, an image by Max F. Klepper, popular military illustrator of the period. The Confederates retreated, leaving two field pieces in Federal hands. Forrest was more angered by the loss of the guns than the retreat of his men.

Far right: Painting of young Emma Sansom mounted behind General Forrest, another work by Max F. Klepper. The girl volunteered, against her mother's advice, to lead the Confederates to the hidden ford at the risk of her life reportedly under fire from the Union rear guard.

Above: Engraving of Captain William B. Forrest, younger brother of General Forrest. Captain Forrest was killed April 30, 1863, leading Confederate elements against Streight's rear guard at Sand Mountain, near Day's Gap.

Dodge demonstrated east toward Courtland to keep the probing Confederates occupied, while Streight and his men turned south toward Russellville and then east to Moulton.

Confederate General Nathan Bedford Forrest and 1,200 of his cavalry had been shadowing the Federals and perceived the division of forces. Forrest interposed his cavalry between the two Union forces and detached elements to harass Dodge, who promptly retired to Corinth, leaving Streight on his own.

Heavy rain and almost impassable roads slowed Streight's party, such that the mules and his still-dismounted men were strung out for miles. Forrest's Confederates began a relentless pursuit of Streight that continued for five grueling days and nights. The rebel general developed a strategy of resting most of his men while small elements constantly kept pressure on the Federals. At every opportunity Forrest also used his artillery as offensive weapons, pushing the guns forward to support his assaults. The Federal flankers and rear guard fended off repeated probes, and the movement became a constant running skirmish, a grueling race of endurance.

Streight passed through Day's Gap at Sand Mountain and engaged Forrest's pesky advance party on the morning of April 29, then disengaged and continued east. But the Southerners knew exactly where he was and where he was going because the mules' braying was heard for miles. A running skirmish continued to Hog Mountain and on to Blountsville. By the next day many mules had died, leaving exhausted men trudging along on foot. Streight's rear guard was attacked as the soldiers moved out toward Gadsden, with continuous skirmishing to the east branch of the Black Warrior River. Elements of Streight's command made a stand at every creek or stream and burnt every bridge, while Forrest persistently ordered his men and guns forward.

Most of Streight's men crossed Black Creek during the morning of May 2 and destroyed the bridge, then continued toward Gadsden. But the command was disintegrating from fatigue. Forrest was shown a hidden ford above the bridge by a local teenage girl, who rode behind Forrest to the spot under fire from the Yankee rear guard. She pointed out the ford, and the legend of Emma Sansom was born. Streight was forced to halt to feed men and animals at Blount's Plantation less than twenty miles from Rome, but the end was near. The men and animals could hardly move and were unable to stay awake long enough even to eat.

Forrest's force, reduced to less than 600 men, ran Streight's raiders to ground near

Cedar Bluff, Alabama, on May 3. The smaller Rebel force confronted Streight's worn-out command and demanded the Federals' surrender. Streight and his officers agreed to a parley. Forrest, with great bravado, arranged to have his two remaining guns pass repeatedly in Streight's view, and made a show of issuing orders to nonexistent units.

The Union Colonel believed he faced a greatly superior force. Forrest told Streight, "I've got enough men to whip you out of your boots." The bold bluff worked and Streight ordered arms stacked in an open field. Only after Forrest had advanced his artillery to cover the prisoners did he expose his small number of men to gather the arms. Streight became apoplectic when he realized he had been deceived, and demanded he be allowed to retrieve his weapons and fight it out. Forrest politely demurred, saying, "All is fair in love and war."

Federal casualties were 12 killed, 69 wounded and 1,466 missing or captured, almost Streight's whole command. Instances of a force outnumbered almost three to one capturing the superior force are notably rare. General Forrest relished repeating the story of Streight's surrender for the rest of his life.

Abel Streight became a prisoner of war in Richmond for ten months until he and 107 other Union prisoners tunneled their way out of Libby Prison in early 1864, one of the great escapes of the war. He retired from the army in 1865 with the rank of brevet brigadier general. He is still remembered in Alabama as the leader of the "Jackass Cavalry."

Emma Sansom became the heroine of Alabama in postwar years, even though she moved to Texas. Her story was included in the 1914 publication by Chapple Publishing Company, *Wizards of the Saddle*, by Bennett H. Young, coincidentally the leader of the St. Albans Raid. She is remembered today by an imposing granite monument in downtown Gadsden, and the Emma Sansom High School.

Below left: Photograph of Emma Sansom taken three years after she led General Forrest to the ford on Black Creek. She became a southern Joan of Arc in Cullman County, Alabama, in the years after the war, and is still remembered there today.

Below: Statue of the teenage heroine Emma Sansom near the bank of the Coosa River at Gadsden, Alabama. She led Forrest and his cavalry to a nearby hidden ford above a bridge burned by the fleeing Union raiders, saving Forrest's troopers a three-hour detour in their pursuit of Streight and his mule-mounted men.

Grierson's Horse Soldiers

Above: Colonel Benjamin H. Grierson, commander of one of the most successful raids of the Civil War. His exploits earned him promotion to brigadier general and subsequently major general. An excellent career officer, he remained in service until 1890.

In contrast to the dismal failure of Streight's effort was the concurrent raid led by Federal Colonel Benjamin H. Grierson. This raid, another diversion in Grant's grand strategy to take Vicksburg, started from LaGrange, Tennessee, on April 17 and terminated in Baton Rouge, Louisiana, on May 2, 1863. Grierson's mission was to cut Vicksburg Railroad, the major east-west supply line from Meridian to the Confederate Gibraltar on the Mississippi. To accomplish this mission, Grierson had to lead his command through the length of the state of Mississippi. General Sherman characterized the operation as "the most brilliant expedition of the Civil War."

General Grant notified Major General Stephen A. Hurlburt, commander of the XVI Army Corps, Department of the Tennessee, headquartered in Memphis, Tennessee, of his plans in early February 1863 and repeatedly mentioned Grierson by name. Hurlburt eventually got the message and ordered Brigadier General William Sooy Smith, commanding at LaGrange, to order Grierson to mount the raid. At the time, Grierson was commanding the First Brigade, First Cavalry Division.

The units Grierson took on the raid were the 6th and 7th Illinois Cavalry, 2nd Iowa Cavalry, with Smith's Section A of Battery K, 1st Illinois Artillery, for artillery support, a force of approximately 1,700 well seasoned, veteran troops. Their mounts were dark-colored geldings, fresh from the remount station at St. Louis. The cavalrymen carried revolvers and breech-loading Sharps and Gywn and Campbell carbines. The Illinois artillerymen were armed with an unusual rifled gun, the small two-pounder wrought iron Woodruff gun, manufactured by the Greenleaf Foundry in Quincy, Illinois. Arms, equipment, men and mounts were all first rate.

The operation began on a pleasant spring morning. Grierson's column of cavalry rode comfortably and unopposed for thirty miles

Above: Some elements of Grierson's 6th Illinois Cavalry were armed with the Model 1859 Sharps Carbine, the most extensively used single-shot carbine of the war. The .52 caliber breechloader was as tough and dependable as the Federal troopers who carried it.

Above right: Unfired Sharps bullets recovered from campsites of elements of the 6th Illinois Cavalry at LaGrange, Tennessee. These bullets are from cartridges that were probably lost or discarded because of damage.

Above: Other elements of the 6th Illinois Cavalry carried the much less popular Cosmopolitan Carbine. This weapon was not as reliable as the Sharps and, although both .52 caliber, ammunition for the two carbines was unfortunately not interchangeable.

Above right: Dropped Cosmopolitan bullet recovered in the same approximate area at LaGrange, Tennessee. Grierson's command used this area as a marshaling point prior to departure on the fabled raid through Mississippi.

Above: Excavated horse curry comb from the campsite of Grierson's cavalry at LaGrange, Tennessee. The wooden handle has deteriorated. This particular type is known as the "fat lady" pattern because of the outline of the metal reinforcement on the back of the comb.

and bivouacked on the Ellis Plantation, just north of Ripley. The next day the Federals crossed the Tallahatchie River, marching in three parallel columns. One column skirmished with Southern forces near New Albany. The following day the three elements rejoined and galloped into Pontotoc, routing the local state troops. They had penetrated seventy miles with no casualties. The next morning Grierson ordered the sick and lame to form a "Quinine Brigade" and retrace their route of march north to LaGrange. He sent another element east to cut the Mobile & Ohio Railroad and then turn north toward LaGrange while the main party, reduced to 950 riders, continued south to Starkville and on to Louisville.

Realizing there was organized Confederate pursuit, Grierson sent another diversionary force east to strike the Mobile & Ohio at Macon while the main force continued south to Philadelphia. Grierson and the main force assaulted the primary objective at Newton Station early the morning of April 24 and destroyed two locomotives and twenty-five boxcars full of commissary and ordnance sup-

plies destined for the Vicksburg garrison – a complete success. The cavalrymen then rode the whole day, camping at the Mackadora Plantation, some fifty miles from the morning victory, after forty hours without rest.

The Yankees, their primary mission completed, turned southwest across the Pearl River toward Hazlehurst where they burned another train, destroyed track and cut telegraph wires. At Union Church, the Federal raiders had their first serious engagement with some regular infantry and Mississippi cavalry under Colonel William Wirt Adams. The fight raged around the church and cemetery and Smith made good use of his little Woodruff guns. The next day the Yankees slipped away south toward Brookhaven and destroyed more rolling stock at Bogue Chitoo Station and again at Summit, dogged all the while by increasing Confederate pursuit.

Finally, at Wall's Bridge on the Tickfaw River, two miles from the Louisiana line, the 9th Louisiana Partisan Rangers and elements of the 9th Tennessee Cavalry, some 115 Southerners, got in front of Grierson. The Woodruff

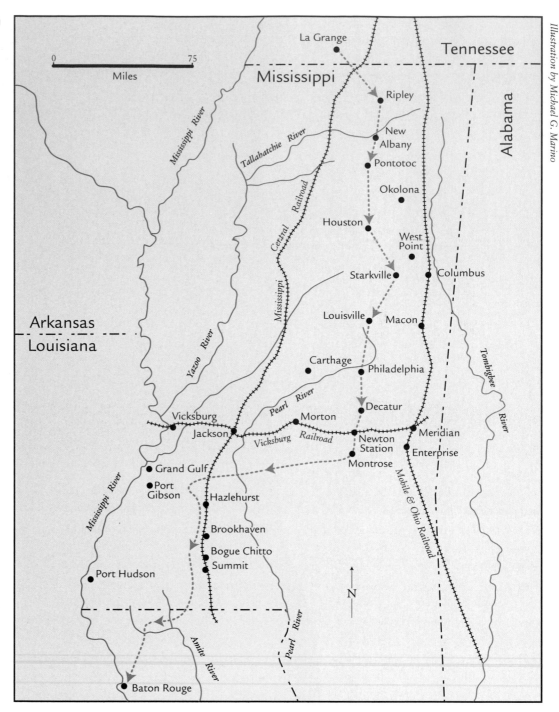

Right: Grierson's route of march from LaGrange to Baton Rouge.

Illustration by Michael G. Marino

guns were used again and a bold charge of the 6th Illinois troopers scattered the Confederates. One Federal soldier was killed and five wounded, two mortally, including Lieutenant Colonel William Blackburn, 7th Illinois; five were captured.

The tired Federals kept in the saddle and crossed the Amite River at Williams Bridge, the last obstacle before Baton Rouge. The raiders covered the last seventy-eight exhausting miles in just twenty-eight hours, most of the time spent consistently in the saddle because cavalrymen in gray were just behind them. Some of the exhausted, half-comatose riders tied their ankles together beneath their mounts' bellies so that they could not fall off. The raiders reached safety and bivouacked at a plantation six miles north of the town. The next day, the whole ragged and muddy command, including Confederate prisoners and 300 liberated slaves, a parade two miles long, moved through Baton Rouge to the hysterical cheers of a flag-waving crowd.

Grierson and his men had covered more than 600 miles between LaGrange and Baton Rouge in sixteen days with very little rest. Amazingly, their total casualties were only thirty-six men. The raiders captured 500 Confederates and killed or wounded an estimated hundred more. They also tore up over fifty miles of railroad track and adjacent telegraph wire, destroyed more than 3,000 small arms and thousands of dollars' worth of supplies and property, and captured over 1,000 horses and mules. Furthermore, for just over a fortnight these 1,700 raiders tied up all of the cavalry and most of the strategic reserve of General Pemberton, commander of Southern forces in Mississippi.

One of the raiders, Sgt. Stephen Forbes, gave a wonderful description of a successful cavalry operation. He said a cavalry raid is a game of rapid march, subtle ruse, gallant dash, sudden surprise and quick and cunning retreat which leaves one's opponent miles in the rear before he knows the fight is over. This was a textbook model of a successful raid from start to finish.

The drama and heroism of this raid were depicted in the 1959 Hollywood classic, *The Horse Soldiers*, a fictionalized film produced by John Ford and starring John Wayne and William Holden as the primary characters, with a number of regular Wayne standby supporting actors. The names of the characters were changed, as were the regiments involved, but the screenplay closely followed the actual raid with some embellishments to add to the excitement. Uniforms, weapons and accouter-

ments were inaccurate, but the movie was a great epic in the Ford/Wayne tradition.

One surviving example of the extremely rare Woodruff rifle is in the artillery collection at the United States Military Academy at West Point, New York.

Above: An exhausted and doleful-appearing Colonel Grierson, seated with chin in hand, rests with his officers at Baton Rouge. Brigadier General Albert L. Lee, wearing a jaunty civilian straw hat, is seated to the far left.

Left: Elements of Grierson's command just arrived at Baton Rouge after marching the length of Mississippi. A Confederate secret service agent named Lytle made the photograph of the still-mounted horsemen, an early example of remarkable covert surveillance.

Cavalry Target: Jeff Davis

If any raid could have changed the course of the war, the Dahlgren-Kilpatrick raid on Richmond might have done it. Unfortunately, it brought the distasteful specter of total war and political assassination to the forefront when wars were still fought with some modicum of chivalry. The incident outraged leaders on both sides at the time, and ominously foretold of the future.

Hugh Judson Kilpatrick, West Point, 1861, was one of the more despicable general officers of the Civil War. Besides being a recognized self-promoter and liar, he also proved himself a thief and coward on numerous occasions. He excelled in the company of loose women and common prostitutes, even during his marriages. It is a minor miracle that he was not dismissed from service for conduct unbecoming an officer on multiple occasions.

Kilpatrick's career was at a new low in mid-October 1863 and he desperately needed a spectacular victory to redeem his badly tarnished reputation. He grasped at a plan sent to Federal authorities by Elizabeth "Crazy Bet" Van Lew, a Federal spy in Richmond, who provided information about Union prisoners of war and local troop dispositions. She reported that 1,000 officers were held at Libby, 6,300 enlisted men at Belle Isle, and that 4,300 others were scattered around town. She indicated that defensive forces were no more than a light screen of home guard troops, and recommended a raid on Richmond. Kilpatrick presented the plan as his own, bypassed the chain of command, and induced President Lincoln to authorize a raid on the Confederate capital. Kilpatrick was thrilled to have young Colonel Ulric Dahlgren as part of the force

Right: Major General Hugh Judson Kilpatrick. Known as "Kil-cavalry" for his typically uncaring disdain for his men and mounts, this academy graduate earned and maintained an unsavory reputation throughout his career. His indecisiveness, possibly cowardice, at the gates of Richmond contributed greatly toward the failure of this raid that could have drastically changed the course of the war.

Center: A postwar view of Libby Prison, the single most photographed building in the defeated Confederacy. Like other Richmond prisons, this site originally had been a warehouse and ship chandlery owned by Libby & Son. Hastily modified to house Federal officers, it was another of the primary targets of the raid.

Left: Libby Prison sat on the bank of the James River. This view shows the rear of the warehouse complex with bars on most of the windows. Colonel Abel Streight was a member of the group of officers that tunneled out of Libby in one of the great mass escapes of the war.

because this famous and respected family name added prestige to the operation.

The acknowledged objective of the mission was the liberation of Union prisoners of war held in and around Richmond. The secret objective was the assassination or capture of President Jefferson Davis and the Confederate cabinet, and the sacking of the city. Dahlgren had a written copy of these plans for the operation that he said "if successful will be the grandest thing on record."

The execution of the mission consisted of a pincer movement, two simultaneous assaults by columns from two different directions. Kilpatrick with the main force would attack down the Brook Pike and enter the city from

the north, while Dahlgren, with a smaller force, would cross the James River and come up from the south into the city. For the raid Kilpatrick selected only the best mounted and outfitted men from his command. To further antagonize his immediate superior, General Alfred Pleasonton, whom he had already bypassed with his outrageous plan, he bet the general "$5,000 that I enter Richmond." Many senior officers of the Army of the Potomac gleefully awaited his failure.

The combined force of Kilpatrick and Dahlgren crossed the Rapidan River at Ely's Ford on the evening of February 28, 1864. The force was just over 4,000 blue cavalrymen supported by six cannons, six ambulances and

Left: Ulric Dahlgren, son of Admiral John A. Dahlgren, shown here in the uniform of a captain. A brave, adventuresome young man, he was severely wounded during the Gettysburg Campaign and lost a leg. Promoted to colonel, he led a detached strike force in the ill-fated raid on Richmond. Documents found on his body indicated one of the mission objectives was the assassination or capture of Davis and members of the Confederate cabinet, vehemently denied by Federal authorities in the aftermath of the raid.

Right: Routes of march of Dahlgren and Kilpatrick elements toward Richmond.

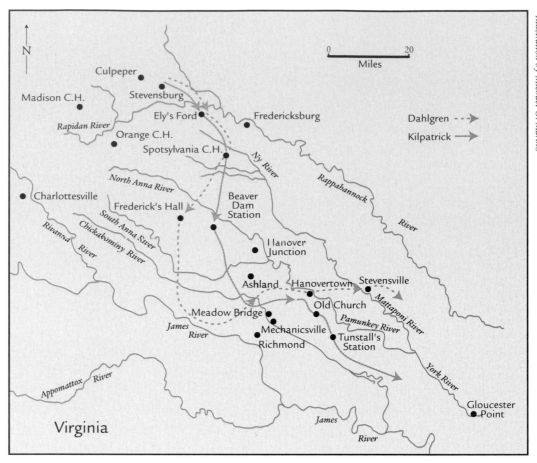

Illustration by Michael G. Marino

Below: The holding pen for Union enlisted prisoners was on Belle Isle, located in the James River, seen in this image. There were no permanent or even temporary structures on the island, so the lack of shelter for the unfortunate soldiers meant they sweltered in the summer and froze in the winter. This site was another objective of the men riding with Dahlgren and Kilpatrick.

three wagons. Confederate scouts quickly reported the movement to General Wade Hampton, on duty with his cavalry at Milford Station on the Richmond, Fredericksburg & Potomac Railroad.

The Union column made good time to Spotsylvania Court House where 460 men under Colonel Dahlgren detached from the main force, swung southwest and headed for the James River. Kilpatrick with the main force rode steadily, crossed the Po River, and contin-

ued through Mt. Pleasant, across the North Anna and on to Beaver Dam Station on the Virginia Central Railroad. Arrogant Kilpatrick sent General Pleasonton an offer to double their bet. He tried to communicate with Dahlgren without success. Kilpatrick skirmished with some Confederates at Ashland and reached the outer ring of defenses around Richmond mid-morning on March 1, exactly on schedule.

Kilpatrick easily penetrated to the intermediate defenses by early afternoon, encountering only token resistance from home guard units until they came under effective artillery fire and Kilpatrick stopped. He had still heard nothing from Dahlgren. The cowardly Kilpatrick quickly decided that the fortifications were too strong, abandoned his plan, and headed posthaste toward Federal lines and safety southeast of the city.

By about 10:00 PM Kilpatrick had recovered his nerve and decided to attempt to enter Richmond down the Mechanicsville Road, but this idea was banished by Wade Hampton and 300 Confederate cavalrymen who had ridden for twenty-five hours to catch the Union braggart. In the dark Hampton's men struck the rear of the greatly superior Federal force and drove them pell mell. The Federals rode through Old Church and Tunstall's Station, harassed all the way by trailing Confederates, and arrived at General Butler's Yorktown Headquarters on March 4.

Dahlgren in the meantime, led by a Negro guide, had bumbled through the countryside in pouring rain, and when he reached the James on the morning of March found it unfordable. In a fit of anger he hanged the guide beside the road and headed for the city down the north side of the James.

Dahlgren's party became strung out along the route as they galloped toward Richmond. He was unaware that his commander no longer supported his movements. The young colonel and fewer than a hundred troopers blundered past Stevensville near King and Queen Court House, straight into a night ambush set by some 9th Virginia Cavalry troops on furlough in the area and a local home guard unit.

Dahlgren was killed in the melee. A thirteen-year-old member of the local unit found the damning papers on Dahlgren's body, and they were passed up the chain of command to General Fitzhugh Lee and on to President Davis. The papers absolutely confirmed that Davis and his cabinet had been targeted for assassination.

A heated diplomatic exchange between General Robert E. Lee and Major General George Gordon Meade followed, with Lee

Left: The Confederate White House, the home of President Jefferson Davis on the corner of 12th and K (now Clay) Streets in Richmond. Originally built in 1818 and refurbished in 1857, the home became the Executive Mansion in 1861. The Federal raiders led by Dahlgren and Kilpatrick hoped to find Davis here, but their plans were foiled and none of the raiders managed to enter the city.

specifically asking if the plot had government sanction. Meade suspected Kilpatrick was the originator but "Kil-cavalry" flatly denied involvement, and Meade passed on the denial to the Confederate leader. The blame fell on the dead and conveniently silent Dahlgren. General Lee quashed recommendations that Federal soldiers who had been captured in the Confederate ambush be executed.

No amount of obfuscation could save Kilpatrick this time, however. He was relieved, demoted and transferred out of the Army of the Potomac. General William T. Sherman, commanding the Military Division of the Mississippi, who shared his vision of total war, accepted him into his command.

As heinous as the plan was, had the President of the Confederate States of America and his cabinet been killed or captured, it most certainly would have brought the war to an abrupt conclusion, and probably would have led to a different format of Reconstruction.

Left: Castle Thunder was one of the numerous "make do" sites used to house prisoners of war in Richmond. Nothing more than a modified three-story warehouse and constantly overcrowded, it was one of the targets of the raid. Freed prisoners were supposed to support the raid, although little thought was given to how they would get arms to do so.

Sheridan's Richmond Raid

Below: Major General Philip Henry Sheridan and his generals. Sheridan stands to the far left. Brigadier General James William Forsyth, Chief of Staff, stands with his hand in his blouse, boyish Major General Wesley Merritt is seated center, acting Brigadier General Thomas Casimer Devin stands, and seated is the ever-flamboyant George A. Custer.

Below right: Brigadier General Alfred Pleasonton. He was promoted to the rank of major general after the superior performance of Federal cavalry under his command against Stuart's cavalry at Brandy Station on June 9, 1863. He commanded the cavalry of the Army of the Potomac but his vocal disapproval of the Kilpatrick-Dahlgren operation resulted in his transfer to the Department of Missouri in March 1864, and the ascendancy of Phil Sheridan.

Confederate cavalry had exhibited marked superiority over their Union counterparts since the beginning of the war but, by the third year, the Federal cavalry had learned many hard and costly lessons. The new commander of the Cavalry Corps of the Army of the Potomac, Major General Philip Henry Sheridan, convinced General Grant that the Union cavalry was ready to confront Stuart's vaunted gray riders on equal terms. Sheridan allowed that, given the chance, he could "whip Stuart." Sheridan's raid on Richmond was to prove this was not an idle boast.

Sheridan's plain and simple mission was to force Stuart to fight. He felt a massive mounted assault on the Confederate capital was the best way to draw his adversary out. He expected Stuart to interpose the cavalry of the Army of Northern Virginia between his forces and Richmond. Sheridan, with three divisions commanded by Generals Wesley Merritt, James E. Wilson and David M. Gregg, some 10,000 Federal cavalry, supported by six bat-

teries of horse artillery, set out May 9, 1864, from Spotsylvania in a southeasterly direction toward the Fredericksburg-Richmond Telegraph Road. The long blue column stretched thirteen miles and moved at an easy, steady walk to insure that the men reached their objective rested, ready and able to fight. The Federals rode to Jerrold's Mill where the Telegraph Road crossed the Ta River, and then southwest through Chilesburg and across the North Anna River to Beaver Dam Station on the Virginia Central Railroad. They encountered only scattered Confederate scouts and pickets.

Brigadier General George A. Custer's brigade was in the lead when they reached Beaver Dam Station in the midst of a crashing thunderstorm. Custer freed nearly four hundred Union prisoners of war, captured two trains and a depot overflowing with quartermaster and medical supplies. He burned the trains, station, all the outbuildings, an estimated 1,500,000 rations and all the medical supplies. The Federals spent the night there

Left: The still-smoking ruins of the Richmond, Fredericksburg & Potomac bridge over the North Anna are stark evidence of the continual havoc wreaked on railroads in all theaters of the war. Sheridan's troopers destroyed the bridges over the North Anna and South Anna Rivers and more than five miles of track on this particular raid.

Far left: George Armstrong Custer, mounted, in the field, in early 1863 before his meteoric rise in rank from company grade officer to general officer. Even then Custer exuded confidence astride a strong, fine-looking horse.

and the next morning, May 10, the entire division destroyed about ten miles of track before continuing the march.

On the second day Confederate forces began to pick at the Federal rear guard, Davies' brigade of Gregg's Division. Brigadier Williams C. Wickham's brigade caught up with the Federal rear guard still at Jerrold's Mill and later at Mitchell's Shop. Stuart, with the brigades of Wickham, Brigadier Lindsay L. Lomax and James B. Gordon, about 4,500 troopers, managed a serious assault on the Federal column at the crossing of the North Anna River.

Sheridan was not distracted, and continued the march southeast, crossing the South Anna at Ground Squirrel Bridge with Lomax's

Brigade hounding his rear. Stuart anticipated Sheridan's objective and raced ahead with his two other brigades to get between Sheridan and Richmond. Stuart rested very briefly at Hanover Junction and reached Yellow Tavern on May 11 about 10:00 AM, his horses and men exhausted.

Yellow Tavern was just two miles north of the outer defense line at the beginning of the Brook Pike that ran into Richmond. Stuart had 3,000 troopers with him and he realized he must fight a defensive action against Sheridan's much superior force, a drastic change from offensive action to which the Southern cavalry was accustomed. The gray troopers had two options: they could face Sheridan's larger force head-on and be overrun, or take them by the flank and hope to divert them from going into the capital. Either way the Confederate cavalry assumed a defensive posture. Stuart chose the latter and a substantial number of Confederate cavalry fought dismounted. This further reduced their number because the horse holders went to the rear.

The action began about 11:00 AM and continued until about 2:00 PM, when there was a momentary lull. By then most of Sheridan's troopers were up with Custer's brigade on the right of the Union line. Custer led a conventional mounted charge of the 5th and 6th Michigan Cavalry in a column against the flank of the Confederates, supported by a frontal assault of two regiments of dismounted Federals. Union troopers armed with Spencer repeating carbines and Sharps breechloading

Left: Major General George Armstrong Custer in all his martial finery. No doubt he wears his signature red tie and custom-tailored frock coat. In spite of his vain and dandy appearance, he was fearless, even foolhardy, in combat and that probably contributed to his death at Little Bighorn after the war.

Right: Major General J. E. B. Stuart carried a 1st Model LeMat Revolver. This massive weapon had a nine-shot .42 caliber cylinder that revolved around a 20-gauge shotgun barrel that served as the cylinder pin; it could be fired by dropping the face of the hammer. The weapon was popular with army and navy personnel. A number were imported through tho blockade.

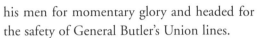
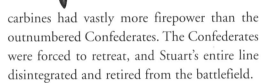

Below: Marker at the grave of General J. E. B. Stuart near Richmond, as it appeared near the close of the war. With the death of Stuart at Yellow Tavern the South lost its most charismatic cavalry leader. His death had a noticeable effect on Southern morale.

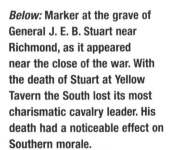

carbines had vastly more firepower than the outnumbered Confederates. The Confederates were forced to retreat, and Stuart's entire line disintegrated and retired from the battlefield.

Stuart tried to rally the folding left flank of Lomax's line as the two Michigan regiments galloped around him and a small group of staff officers. The 1st Virginia Cavalry countercharged and, in the midst of the swirling action, Private John A. Huff, Company E, 5th Michigan Cavalry, who was retreating on foot toward his lines, turned and shot the Confederate general with his revolver, mortally wounding him.

Sheridan knew he had won the battle and was smart enough to realize that, although he could ride into Richmond, he could not hold the city. He wisely decided against sacrificing his men for momentary glory and headed for the safety of General Butler's Union lines.

The Federals began the march to Haxall's Landing in a horrible storm before midnight. Along the way they encountered "torpedoes," buried artillery shells with trip wires attached. The Federals brought Confederate prisoners to the head of the column and made them crawl on their hands and knees in the darkness to disarm the "infernal machines." They finally crossed Meadow Bridge and arrived at Butler's positions, and subsequently rejoined the Army of the Potomac near Spotsylvania in late May. Federal forces had 625 casualties but they released nearly 400 prisoners and captured some 300 Confederates while destroying tens of thousands of dollars' worth of irreplaceable supplies and equipment.

The greatest Confederate loss of the day was General Stuart. His service to the Army of Northern Virginia was invaluable and his victories had bolstered Southern morale on many occasions. His death, together with that of General Jackson, cast a blanket of gloom over the Confederacy. General Lee subsequently appointed veteran General Wade Hampton to command the cavalry, but it was never the same.

Yellow Tavern was the first unequivocal complete Federal victory, and it was Sheridan's first independent command as a cavalry leader, at which he proved extremely competent. From this point forward there was no questioning the superiority of Federal cavalry. The use of cavalry had matured greatly and it became commonplace for the men to ride to battle and then fight dismounted, as General Forrest had been doing in the west all along.

Above: At the end of the long ride, after the fight at Yellow Tavern and the whisker-close approach to Richmond, Sheridan's played-out riders are pictured crossing the Chesterfield Bridge on the way to safety within the lines of General Benjamin Butler on May 24, 1864.

Left: Only the scorched trucks of the burned cars remain next to the shattered ruins of the station complex. Sheridan and his men were past masters at laying waste to anything of value to the Confederates, be it military or civilian property, that came within reach.

Hunter's Shenandoah Raid

Right: David Hunter is a good example of the type of inept officer unfortunately appointed by President Lincoln early in the war. He had little military ability and was a petty, vengeful individual. Luckily for Federal forces, his disasters were relatively small ones and he was finally relegated to commands where he could do little damage. He is remembered as one of the villains of the Civil War…by both sides.

Right: Brigadier General William Edmondson "Grumble" Jones had been colonel of the 7th Virginia Cavalry and served under General Stuart at Brandy Station. Jones tried to protect Staunton, Virginia, from Hunter but his small force was defeated at Piedmont on June 5 and Jones was killed. Crook shortly joined Hunter to begin the systematic devastation of the valley.

Grant began a major offensive in the spring of 1864. Major General Franz Sigel, with 6,500 troops, was ordered to clear the Shenandoah Valley of Confederate forces. Sigel faced Major General John C. Breckenridge, whose scratch force included two hard-used infantry brigades, a cavalry brigade, local militia and teenage cadets from the Virginia Military Institute in Lexington, Virginia, possibly 5,000 men.

Sigel marched up the valley to New Market, constantly harassed by Confederate cavalry, and confronted the gray troops just north of the village on Sunday, May 15. The Federals formed a commanding defensive line with twenty-eight pieces of artillery. Breckenridge ordered his outnumbered troops, including the cadets, to attack with the words, "Put the boys in." The Confederate troops swept the Union position and the brave cadets captured some guns, losing ten killed or mortally wounded and forty-seven wounded. Union forces withdrew from the valley and the little German was relieved four days later. The young cadets from Lexington were the heroes of the battle.

Sigel joined the growing list of Federal generals beaten by Confederate forces in the Shenandoah Valley. Sigel, an inept general but the darling of the large German-American community, was replaced on May 21, 1864, by General David Hunter, West Point, Class of 1822. Hunter had no sterling record himself. He had been in command of the Department of the South and in overall command of operations around Secessionville, South Carolina. A reconnaissance in force met with disaster on June 16, 1862, and the subordinate commander, General Benham, was allowed to resign from service. Hunter was relieved of duty and was idle and available, "awaiting orders."

Hunter assumed command of the Department of West Virginia and was told to clear

the valley of Confederate forces. His mission was to destroy the Virginia Central Railroad, the James River Canal and commerce in the grain basket of the Valley, and then join Grant

also the home of John Letcher, governor of the state. Confederate General John McCausland had three regiments of cavalry, the 8th, 16th and 17th Virginia. They numbered only 1,500 men but they did their best. They burned bridges and obstructed the road with downed trees to slow the Federals, but were vastly outnumbered and pushed aside.

in the east. Grant specifically ordered him to advance on Staunton and then cross the Blue Ridge Mountains and attack Charlottesville and Gordonsville.

After New Market, Lee felt comfortable transferring Major General Breckenridge and his infantry to the Richmond area. The defense of the Shenandoah was left to Brigadier General William "Grumble" Jones and 8,500 veteran troops, a combined cavalry and infantry command.

Hunter, with a force of 8,500 men, started up the Valley on May 26. Grant also ordered Brigadier General George Crook, with 10,000 men, to support Hunter in his efforts, giving the Federals nearly 20,000 men to confront a much smaller Confederate threat. Hunter's command took the Valley Pike to Harrisonburg and then headed east. The command ran into "Grumble" Jones and 5,000 troops at Piedmont, June 5, 1864, and after ten hours of skirmishing and charge and countercharge, Federal cavalry hit the gray right flank and the line broke. The defeat turned into a rout and the Federals captured nearly 1,000 Confederates and killed or wounded about 600. General Jones was killed trying to rally his troops. Hunter had fewer than 800 killed and wounded, a decided victory.

The Federals entered Staunton, Virginia, on June 6 and set about destroying everything in sight with a vengeance. They wrecked ten miles of Central Virginia railroad track, the arsenal and depot. Crook belatedly joined Hunter on June 8 and on June 10 the combined Federal force headed south toward Lynchburg.

Lexington, Virginia, lay on Hunter's route of march. The small town was the site of the Virginia Military Institute, whose teenage cadets had played a significant role in the defeat of General Sigel at New Market. It was

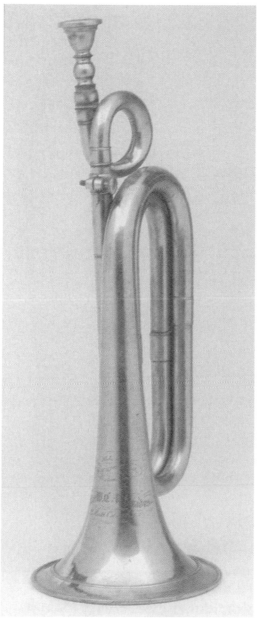

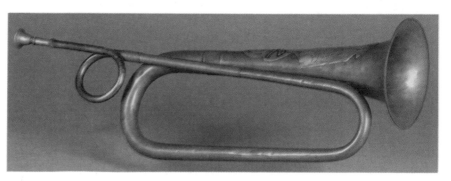

Left: Brigadier General George Crook, shown here as a major general, supported Hunter's depredations in the Shenandoah Valley. He suffered the humiliation of being captured by McNeill's Partisan Rangers at Cumberland, Maryland, in February 1865. Crook was headquartered at the Revere House, owned by a Mr. Dailey who had a daughter, Mary, and a son. The son served with McNeill's unit and General Crook later married Mary.

Left: Unit control has always been an essential aspect of war. In the often fast-moving combat employed by mounted raiders and cavalry units, split-second execution of movements was necessary. Bugles such as this German silver example communicated orders through recognized calls. When stealth and secrecy were required the bugle obviously was not the method of communication used.

Below: Commands were transmitted by bugle call in mounted units. In the melee of combat, when voice commands could not be heard, the appropriate commands to advance, charge or retreat were sounded by the unit bugler on order of the commanding officer. This brass bugle is a configuration that was commonly used during the war.

Right: General Hunter was well aware that cadets from the Virginia Military Institute had been instrumental in defeating his predecessor, General Sigel, at New Market and that General "Stonewall" Jackson had been a professor at the school prior to the war. After Hunter's raiders visited Lexington all that remained of the main barracks of the military school was this burnt-out shell.

The Yankees, while constructing a pontoon bridge across the river just north of town, brought up a section of artillery and amused themselves by shelling the defenseless town and the adjacent school. After occupying the town, Hunter seized the house of Institute Superintendent Francis H. Smith.

The Yankees went on a three-day spree of burning and looting in Rockbridge County that has never been forgotten. Much of the town was put to the torch and Washington College was wrecked, the scientific instruments being destroyed along with many books, and the buildings used for stables. The barracks, mess hall, officers' quarters and the library with 10,000 volumes at the Virginia Military Institute were burned. Even the bronze statue of George Washington that overlooked the parade ground was seized and carried off. The home of Governor John Letcher of Virginia was burned to the ground. The women and children present were not even allowed to remove furniture or personal belongings. At some point during the conflagration Hunter said, "Doesn't it burn beautifully." An estimated two million dollars in damage was done to property of questionable military significance.

After pillaging Lexington, Hunter and his soldiers marched toward Lynchburg, intermittently harassed by outnumbered Confederates. Breckenridge, back from Richmond, held Lynchburg with two under-strength brigades. Meanwhile, Lee had ordered General Jubal Early and his II Corps to travel via Char-

lottesville to Lynchburg to protect the rail center. Early arrived by train around 1:00 PM on June 17, and the gray infantry formed quickly into a line of battle. Hunter and the Federal force arrived later in the afternoon, tired after a hard march.

The Federals shelled the Confederate defensive lines sporadically for the remainder of the day while plans were being made for a major assault the next morning. By the morning of June 18 all of General Early's 8,000 men were in the strong Confederate defensive works ready and waiting for the assault. Hunter's troops made several timid and indecisive probes throughout the day, but these were easily repulsed.

That night Hunter's courage failed him and he began to withdraw. Early's men vigorously pursued Hunter's troops at dawn and chased them to the top of Sweet Spring Mountain. Then the Federal withdrawal disintegrated into a stampede all the way to West Virginia. The Confederates captured nine pieces of artillery and part of the Union wagon trains. Hunter's precipitous withdrawal meant there was no Union force between Early's II Corp and the Federal capital, a gross tactical blunder that did not go unnoticed by General Lee. This set the stage for Jubal Early's dash down the Valley and raid on Washington that very easily could have tipped the war in the favor of the South.

Hunter subsequently met with his commanding officers. After seeing Generals Grant and Sheridan, Hunter was relieved at his own request and spent the rest of the war "awaiting orders" once again. There are no records of what other options were offered. Crook succeeded him in command and suffered the embarrassment of being captured by Confederate raiders in February 1865.

For reasons unknown, Hunter was appointed president of the Military Tribunal that tried and quickly executed the four civilians accused of President Lincoln's assassination. Incredibly, he was brevetted brigadier and major general in the Regular Army but retired from service in 1866, the same year that Washington's statue was returned to VMI.

Hunter is probably best remembered for his depredations in the Shenandoah Valley. The poem, *The Murder of David Creigh*, by Mrs. F. H. Smith, memorializes the execution near Brownsburg of an innocent civilian by General Hunter's orders. The general is also credited with the execution of Captain Matthew X. White who was shot in the back near Lexington. Hunter died in Washington in 1886.

General Philip Sheridan described, evidently with some measure of pride, the desolation in the Shenandoah Valley caused by his troops and those of Hunter. He boasted, "A crow could not fly over it without carrying his rations with him." Neither Sheridan nor Hunter is fondly remembered in the Valley, even after the passage of nearly a century and a half.

Above and left: After Hunter's unsatisfactory performance in the valley Alfred Thomas Archimedes Torbert took over command of the cavalry of the Army of the Shenandoah later in August 1864 to contend with Confederate forces still active in the area. General Torbert's non-regulation blouse and bell-bottomed sailor's trousers rivaled some of the uniforms sported by Custer from time to time.

Sherman's Neckties in Alabama

By mid-summer of 1864 Union General William T. Sherman was heavily committed to the Atlanta Campaign and the capture of the city, a vital railroad hub and ordnance and supply center. Confederate forces had withdrawn to a heavily fortified defensive perimeter but still received supplies and reinforcements by rail from other locations. General Sherman realized this lifeline of the garrison had to be cut in order for the Confederates to be forced to surrender or evacuate.

Major General Lovell Harrison Rousseau was a Kentuckian by birth and not a West Point graduate, but the Federal officer had some native military ability and a good record. At this time he commanded the District of Tennessee headquartered at Nashville. Sherman ordered him to organize a raid into northern Alabama to sever the supply lines to Atlanta. Rousseau developed a plan and, even though he was not a cavalryman, volunteered to lead the raid. Sherman accepted his proposal with some modifications. Rousseau's mission was to destroy the railroads in the area, and cut the one remaining rail connection from Selma Arsenal and supply depots in Montgomery to the Confederate garrison of Atlanta, "doing all the mischief possible" as Sherman put it.

Elements from two seasoned brigades of cavalry, primarily drawn from Judson Kilpatrick's command near Chattanooga, were assigned to General Rousseau for the mission. These units were the 8th Indiana Cavalry, 5th Iowa Cavalry, 2nd Kentucky Cavalry, 9th Ohio Cavalry, 4th Tennessee (Union) Cavalry, and a section of Battery E, 1st Michigan Light Artillery, armed with two 3-inch Parrott Rifles, a total of about 2,500 men. Sherman told Rousseau to concentrate his efforts between Montgomery and Opelika, and if successful continue on to meet his forces in Georgia.

During this operation Rousseau's adversary was Lieutenant General Stephen Dill Lee, West Point, Class of 1854, commanding the Department of Alabama, Mississippi and East Louisiana and scattered troops under his command.

Left: These rails have already been heated and bent but probably not sufficiently deformed to prevent repair and reuse. The soldiers who did this job must have been in a hurry. Eventually, the diabolical Smeed clamps were developed that easily turned rails into huge, useless and irreparable corkscrews.

Far left: General Rousseau was one of the many general officers on both sides who performed their duties faithfully and well throughout the war but never received the public accolades of some of the more flamboyant or newsworthy contemporaries. Regardless of his present anonymity, Harrison Rousseau contributed greatly to Sherman's ultimate success in the Atlanta Campaign.

Left: The stripped railroad bed and rails wrapped around the telegraph pole are grim evidence of the sad destruction of yet another railroad. This type of warfare completely wrecked the Southern railroad system by the end of the war. It took decades for the rail transportation system of the area to be restored.

Above: Various raiders developed railroad wrecking to a fine art. Here, the gathered ties have been neatly stacked and the rails laid across the makeshift pyre. When the middle of the rails became heated to a cherry glow, raiders would grab the ends and wrap the rails around nearby trees or telephone poles.

The newly minted Union cavalry commander started from Decatur, Alabama, on July 10, 1864, and his objective was Montgomery & West Point Railroad. His planned route of march would take him by Sommersville, Blountsville, Asheville, Talladega and Carrollton to Sherman's forces at Marietta, north of Atlanta. The blue cavalrymen reached the Coosa River at Greensport on July 13.

Early the next morning Confederates on the opposite side of the river at Ten Islands Ford, south of Greensport, fired on the Federals. This greatly outnumbered force consisted of about 200 gray-clad troopers, elements of the 6th and 8th Alabama Cavalry, under General James H. Clanton, The Federals forced the crossing with little effort and the Confederates melted away. Part of Rousseau's force subsequently destroyed the Janney Furnace in St. Clair County, Alabama,

which supplied essential material for Selma Arsenal. On July 15 Rousseau occupied Talladega, burned the railroad depot, rolling stock and ordnance facilities, and destroyed a large amount of army food supplies so critical for the Atlanta garrison. Riding on, the Yankee raiders destroyed the Tallassee Armory and at least 500 new carbines just manufactured at that facility.

On July 17 Rousseau's column reached its primary objective, the Montgomery & West Point Railroad, at Loachapoka. The Federal troopers methodically stacked the wooden ties from the railroad bed and set fire to them. Then they laid the metal rails across the burning piles and, when the rails became hot enough, they were twisted so that they could not be re-laid and used again. The end result was what has since become known as "Sherman neckties." The track was destroyed in this manner between Loachapoka and Notasulga, and small local supply depots met the same fate. The next day the Yankees destroyed six more miles of track between Auburn and West Point, Georgia, and fought a small skirmish with a scratch force of invalid Confederate soldiers from the hospital in Auburn who were easily dispersed.

While that small skirmish at Auburn was in progress, a mixed bag of 500 Southern troops confronted Federals at Chewa Station, Georgia. This force was made up of Lockhardt's Battalion of Home Guards, mainly teenage boys, fifty University of Alabama cadets on furlough, and other miscellaneous small units, all poorly armed and equipped but not lacking in bravery. But it was badly beaten.

Rousseau's men spent a total of about thirty-six hours "working on the railroad," and they were very thorough. Eventually they arrived, tired but in high spirits, at their destination near Marietta.

The results of Rousseau's 400-mile ride through Alabama and Georgia were very satisfying for General Sherman. Federal losses were minimal. Only twelve men were killed and thirty wounded, and one of the Parrott Rifles was lost. During the raid, thirty miles of track were destroyed, and it took the Confederates over a month to restore the railroads to some semblance of service. The disruption of delivery of critical war supplies to Atlanta was a great loss to the garrison.

General Rousseau said it was impossible to estimate the value of the enormous amount of supplies destroyed, but noted that at Opelika alone the Federal raiders seized 42,000 pounds of bacon, flour and sugar, and six freight cars of leather. Confederate losses were estimated at about a hundred killed and wounded.

By this time in the Atlanta Campaign the morale of the Confederate defenders had already begun to erode. Rousseau's raid demonstrated conclusively that Federal raiders could penetrate, almost at will, the vacuum that existed within the Confederate states. The interior of Dixieland was undefended, and this

realization was a tremendous blow to shaky Southern confidence.

After the war, Rousseau, a Radical Republican, was elected to Congress from Kentucky, but soon became opposed to the draconian measures of Reconstruction and in favor of moderation. During an emotional discussion in a hallway in the Capitol, he severely beat Josiah B. Grinnell of Iowa, a fellow Radical Republican, and was censured by the House. He resigned, only to be overwhelmingly re-elected to his vacated seat. By 1866 Rousseau had had enough of politics and re-entered the army. President Johnson made him a brevet major general in the Regular Army, and General Rousseau was chosen to formally receive the territory of Alaska from the Russian government in 1867. He died in 1869.

The stone chimney of the Janney Furnace still stands today as a reminder that Rousseau passed that way, and there is a monument to General Rousseau at Cave Hill Cemetery in Louisville, Kentucky, although the general is buried in Arlington National Cemetery. General Rousseau's raid against the Montgomery & West Point Railroad was considered one of the most successful Union cavalry operations of the war.

Above: Sherman's wrecking crew, probably photographed in early 1865. Left to right, one-armed Major General Oliver Otis Howard stands next to seated Major General John Alexander "Black Jack" Logan. Major General William Babcock Hazen served as chief of staff for William Tecumseh Sherman, seated center. Yankee General Jefferson Davis stands with hand in blouse next to seated General Henry Warner Slocum. Major General Joseph Anthony Mower stands far right.

Stoneman's Successes and Failures

Right: George Stoneman was another Federal general who managed to get himself captured by Confederate forces during the war. Although a competent career officer, Stoneman seemed to have plain bad luck on several occasions and had the disadvantage of serving under General Sherman, who cared little for him.

Union officers George Stoneman and George B. McClellan were both West Point graduates, Class of 1846. Stoneman had earlier served under his classmate and was promoted to the rank of brigadier general and chief of cavalry when McClellan took command of the Army of the Potomac in August 1861. After the disastrous Peninsula Campaign, Stoneman was placed in command of the 1st Division, III Corps, but when General Joe Hooker assumed command of the Army of the Potomac on January 26, 1863, he recalled Stoneman as chief of cavalry as part of his subsequent reorganization of the army.

The Chancellorsville Raid

During the Chancellorsville Campaign in April-May 1863, Hooker ordered Stoneman, with almost the entire cavalry corps, to operate aggressively in the rear of Lee's Army of Northern Virginia, thereby effectively depriving the Union Army of its eyes and ears, one of Hooker's multitudes of mistakes. This flawed tactic helped allow Confederate General Jackson's unobserved flank march, and contributed to the resounding Federal defeat.

Both Hooker and Stoneman were relieved after Chancellorsville. Stoneman was replaced by General Alfred Pleasonton, and was relegated to riding a desk as Chief of the Cavalry Bureau in Washington. The following winter he was exiled to the west to command the XXIII Corps. Then, during the Atlanta Campaign that began on May 1, 1864, he was given another chance and led the Cavalry Corps of the Army of the Ohio under Major General Sherman's overall command, but was captured on July 31, 1864.

Right: Brigadier General Alfred Pleasonton did not accompany Stoneman on the Richmond raid but stayed with the army. His repulse of a minor Confederate patrol was somehow embellished into the repulse of General Jackson's 2nd Corps. This exaggerated victory conveniently positioned Pleasonton for promotion to major general and Stoneman's replacement.

Atlanta with McCook, July 26-31, 1864

William Tecumseh Sherman was not particularly impressed with cavalry during the early stages of the Civil War. Federal cavalry was unquestionably inferior to their Southern counterparts, notwithstanding the Union's abundance of advanced weapons and almost unlimited stock of superior horses. Sherman had relegated his mounted troops to the role of substitute infantry during his 1864 campaign, but upon approaching Atlanta he decided to give them one more chance to prove their mettle.

Sherman ordered Major General Stoneman to take his cavalry division, numbering 2,200 riders and 4,500 men of Brigadier General Kenner Garrard's 2nd Cavalry Division, Army of the Cumberland, and probe east of Atlanta. Concurrently, he ordered Brigadier General Edward Moody McCook, with 3,000 men, to probe west of Atlanta. Their objective was to join forces at Lovejoy Station, forty miles south, and destroy the Macon & Western Railroad, the last remaining supply link of Confederate General John Bell Hood's army holding Atlanta. If they could succeed it could force the withdrawal of the Confederate defenders of the city.

Stoneman, looking for some way to redeem his reputation, asked Sherman for authorization to proceed further south after completing the primary mission, in order to liberate 30,000 Federal prisoners of war held at Andersonville and Macon, Georgia. Sherman agreed to Stoneman's suggestion, but stipulated the primary objective was paramount.

Stoneman and McCook launched their raid July 27 but Stoneman immediately disobeyed his orders. While he headed for Andersonville to liberate Union prisoners and cover himself with glory, he left Garrard's division to make the demonstration to Lovejoy Station. Stoneman's departure from the original plan meant that the Federals were moving in three smaller and weaker columns.

Confederate cavalry under General Joseph Wheeler were quick to see an opportunity to attack the isolated Union columns and destroy them piecemeal. On July 28, Wheeler and his

Left: William Woods Averell, seated, as colonel of the 3rd Pennsylvania Cavalry in 1862, was a brigadier general serving under Stoneman during the Chancellorsville Campaign in 1863. General Stoneman and General Averell were involved in the poorly conceived cavalry operations, detached from the army, during this campaign.

Left: Brigadier General David McMurtrie Gregg commanded a division under George Stoneman during the unsuccessful raid on Richmond during the Chancellorsville Campaign, but fortunately the remainder of his service was with other commanders rather than Stoneman. A very competent leader, he mysteriously and abruptly resigned from the service in February 1865.

Left: Brigadier General John Buford, along with Gregg, led elements under Stoneman in the failed raid on Richmond. Buford's exemplary performance was noted even though the operation was unsuccessful. Buford subsequently commanded a cavalry division at Gettysburg and performed brilliantly, but died of typhoid fever before the end of the year.

Right: Major General Edward Moody McCook led supporting elements during Stoneman's abortive Atlanta operations and demonstrated his ability to destroy undefended railroads and civilian property at Lovejoy Station. About 950 Federal troopers of his command were captured before they could rejoin the main force. He resigned from service at the end of the war and was United States minister to Hawaii in 1869 and later territorial governor of Colorado.

Far right: Joe Wheeler was another very talented Confederate cavalry commander. He was promoted from 2nd lieutenant to major general in less than two years and earned every advance in rank. Stoneman had the misfortune of contending with Wheeler and his cavalry during operations around Atlanta.

Below left: After Sherman's forces captured Atlanta, and in preparation for the march to the sea, everything of military value still standing was destroyed. Atlanta as a rail center ceased to exist. The smoking remains of the car sheds of the Western & Atlantic Railroad were mute testimony to efficiency of Yankee rail wreckers.

Below right: Sherman's troops systematically ripped up the rail yards in Atlanta using special horseshoe-shaped clamps invented by E. C. Smeed, an officer who served under Herman Haupt, the brilliant head of the U.S. Military Railroad system. Smeed allegedly said, "I have a thing that will tear up track as quickly as you can say Jack Robinson and spoil rails so nothing but a rolling mill can ever repair them."

men routed Garrard's division at Flatrock Bridge and forced the beaten Federals to retreat back north. Wheeler detailed one brigade to harass Garrard's withdrawal, and took the rest of his force after the remaining two columns of Stoneman and McCook.

McCook managed to reach Lovejoy Station July 29 and spent four hours ravaging the railroad. Elements of Wheeler's cavalry drove him off west toward Newman, where the Yankee raiders were surrounded by five brigades of Confederate cavalry on July 30. McCook ordered his troops to fight their way out independently. Some 750 Federal cavalrymen, two pieces of artillery, the whole pack train, and a considerable number of horses were captured before they could rejoin Sherman's army. More damage was done to civilian homes and private property in the area than to the railroad, which was quickly repaired.

Stoneman reached the outskirts of Macon on July 29 and found the town defended by alerted state troops. He skirted the town to the south and crossed the Ocmulgee River, heading for Andersonville, but at Hillsboro (Sunshine Church) was confronted by three brigades of Confederate cavalry under the command of Brigadier General Alfred Iverson. Stoneman's force, tired and outnumbered, were unable to fight their way out, and

Left: The Union prisoners shown here in the overcrowded prison stockade at Andersonville were the objective of Stoneman when he deliberately disobeyed orders and led his raiders against this secondary objective. Only the fact that Stoneman himself was captured in the attempt and became a prisoner of war saved him from court martial. General Sherman was livid and Stoneman's conduct only added to an already strained relationship.

the disobedient general managed to get himself captured with over 500 of his men on July 31, 1864.

The most spectacular event of the poorly executed raid was the horrendous train wreck at Griswoldville, Georgia, site of the revolver factory. A detachment of the raiders captured a 27-car freight train near the town. The cars were uncoupled and burned where they stood. The raiders put the engine in reverse and opened the throttle, sending the engine careening down the track toward the town. The thundering engine slammed into a passenger train crammed with refugees that had stopped at Griswoldville station. Although the train was destroyed, none of the hysterical passengers was killed, miraculously, although many were injured.

Stoneman's flagrant abuse of his orders, his subsequent capture and the overall failure of the mission bolstered Sherman's disdain for cavalry. The only reason that Sherman did not court martial Stoneman was because he was fortunately out of reach as a prisoner of war. The hapless Stoneman was exchanged in less than ninety days and found himself appointed second in command by his friend, General John Schofield, with the misgivings of Secretary of War Stanton and Generals Grant and Sherman, all of whom had no use for Stoneman whatsoever by this time.

Below: Another view of a section of the critical Atlanta rail yard with cars on tracks of the Western & Atlantic Railroad, literally one of the lifelines of the Confederacy. The loss of rolling stock and railroads crippled the Confederate war effort more than any other one thing, and General Sherman was acutely aware of his ability to strike a major blow in this campaign.

Left: The main train sheds at the Atlanta rail yard, center of the strategic rail junction, one of the main objectives of the Atlanta Campaign. The mission of so many of the raids mounted by both sides was the destruction of means of transportation and communication. Loss of facilities like this deprived the Confederates of the ability to move and supply troops, the ability to make war.

Iron Mines and Salt Works, December 1, 1864-January 1, 1865

Stoneman, more anxious than ever to salvage his battered reputation after his ignominious capture in Georgia, set out in miserable weather from Knoxville, Tennessee, on December 1, 1864. He commanded a force consisting of 4,200 loyal Kentucky cavalrymen led by Brigadier General Stephen G. Burbridge and 1,500 loyal Tennessee cavalrymen led by Brigadier General Alvan Cullem Gillem. Their objective was to wreck the salt and lead mines in Southwest Virginia. The primary target was King's Salt Works in Saltville, Virginia, a major source of salt for the state and the Confederate Quartermaster Department.

Beyond Kingsport, Tennessee, on December 13, Stoneman's raiding party overran an under-strength cavalry brigade, about 800 troopers, commanded by Brigadier General Basil Duke, remnants of General John Hunt Morgan's Kentucky cavalry. Two days later, near Bristol on the Tennessee-Virginia state line, Stoneman's command encountered and routed mounted Confederates under Brigadier General John C. Vaughn. The Federals chased the disorganized and fleeing Confederates east into Virginia, through Marion. The Yankees then turned their attention to the destruction of mines and foundries around Wytheville.

Stoneman's main adversary was Major General John C. Breckenridge, commanding the Department of Southwest Virginia, with about 6,000 men. Stoneman's troops feinted toward the Virginia and Tennessee Railroad and forced Breckenridge to face this new threat. Breckenridge managed to fend off this attack but Stoneman cut him off from Saltville. The Confederate forces were overwhelmed, leaving Saltville virtually undefended. The Saltville Home Guard was made up of 700 hungry, poorly armed old men and young boys, and was quickly dispersed.

The Federals spent the next forty-eight hours thoroughly destroying the salt works by breaking all the salt kettles, smashing the furnaces and drying sheds, ruining some 100,000 bushels of salt, and dumping ordnance down all the wells. The Federals did not molest private property or homes in the area, but they completely destroyed every factory, mill, depot, warehouse, train and bridge along the route of march. The Yankees captured four towns, some 900 prisoners, 3,000 small arms, 19 pieces of artillery, 25,000 rounds of artillery ammunition, and some 3,000 horses and mules. They also confiscated four secession printing presses.

The Federal force retired triumphant in its success without opposition, Burbridge back to Kentucky and Gillem's command to Knoxville, in weather that was incredibly bad. Only 800 of the 4,400 mounts of Burbridge survived the march, and severe frostbite of extremities required many amputations among the men. Nevertheless, this time Stoneman had had some luck and did it all right.

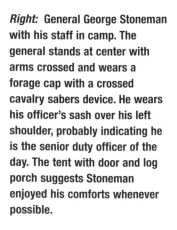

Right: General George Stoneman with his staff in camp. The general stands at center with arms crossed and wears a forage cap with a crossed cavalry sabers device. He wears his officer's sash over his left shoulder, probably indicating he is the senior duty officer of the day. The tent with door and log porch suggests Stoneman enjoyed his comforts whenever possible.

North Carolina, March 20-April 23, 1865

The Confederacy was doomed in 1865, but Sherman's army was still encountering stiff resistance during the march through the Carolinas to join Grant with the Army of the Potomac in Virginia. Grant ordered Major General George H. Thomas, commanding at Nashville, to send some cavalry force into the Carolinas to act as a diversion and take some of the pressure off Sherman's advance. George Stoneman was still basking in the glow of success from his victory at Saltville when he received the call from Sherman, his former commander during the Atlanta Campaign, to give assistance, although Sherman surely remembered poor Stoneman's less-than-stellar performance.

As was apparently common with Stoneman, he had difficulty getting enough horses and Spencer carbines with which to equip his force. Also, the regiments that were designated to make up the force were widely dispersed so it took six weeks to mount the raid. Meanwhile, Grant bombarded General Thomas with wires, demanding situation reports. At the same time, Stoneman sent a stream of excuses as to why he was detained. By the time Stoneman finally rode out of Knoxville on March 20, with a cavalry division under the immediate command of General Gillem, Grant had just about reached the limit of his patience with Stoneman.

Initially, Stoneman was told he would threaten Columbia, South Carolina, but Sherman's hard-fighting army had already laid waste to that place and was already near Goldsboro before Stoneman could get moving. Finally, on March 20, the reluctant Stoneman and his men left Tennessee and rode into the forbidding mountains of North Carolina.

Stoneman had learned some lessons from prior raids and he had only one four-gun battery with caissons, one supply wagon and ten ambulances attached to the whole command. The cavalry could move much faster without the encumbrances of a long train of wheeled carriages to slow them down. They all knew the war was winding down and no one wanted to be the last casualty.

The Federals faced negligible opposition and spent some time destroying 125 miles of track and every bridge and trestle of the East Tennessee & Virginia Railroad between Wytheville and Salem, and the Piedmont Railroad between Danville and Greensborough, even though they well knew that the Confederates had no more rolling stock to use on the track.

The Yankees heard of the surrender of General Lee and the Army of Northern Virginia, and rode on unopposed into Ashville. They continued on to Hendersonville where they learned that General Joseph E. Johnston had surrendered the 30,000 surviving troops of the once-feared Army of Tennessee to Sherman.

Sherman then ordered Stoneman to take his worn-out and disheartened cavalrymen toward Raleigh to interdict the supposed route of escape of the fleeing president of the Confederacy, Jefferson Davis, along with members of his cabinet and escort. The men knew the war was nearly over; the troops knew they were not accomplishing anything; and this detail proved to be another exercise in futility since no contact was made. During two whole weeks of the endeavor the Federals had encountered only small cavalry units and demoralized home guard outfits. Stoneman reported capturing some 2,000 men, most of whom turned themselves in, and destroying some miles of useless railroad track.

George Stoneman's military career was a roller coaster of highs and lows. Undaunted and resilient, he remained on active duty until 1871, when he retired and moved to California where he was successful in civilian life. He served a term as governor of the state from 1882 to 1886, but later moved back to New York near his place of birth, where he died in 1894. Stoneman and Sherman never became friends.

Left: General Stoneman sits far right in front of a tent in a very temporary camp just prior to launching his ill-fated attempt to free Federal prisoners at Andersonville. The general appears to be handing the standing orderly sergeant a document, possibly the alert order for his men to prepare to move out. None of the other soldiers appears to be very eager to go.

The Last Federal Raid

Above right: General August Valentine Kautz augmented Wilson's Third Cavalry Division when they participated in a small raid against the Danville and Southside Railroad in June 1864. Kautz did not perform well but Wilson learned lessons that he would employ the following year. Kautz had the dubious distinction of serving under General David Hunter on the military commission that tried the Lincoln conspirators.

Bottom left: Brigadier General James Harrison Wilson led the last raid of the Civil War. The primary objective was Selma, Alabama, the site of the Selma Arsenal, Selma Naval Gun Foundry and Navy Yard. The Federal raiders captured 288 pieces of artillery and 6,280 Confederate prisoners, including President Jefferson Davis. Wilson served as a general officer during the Spanish American War in 1898 and the 1900 Boxer Rebellion in China. He lived until 1925.

Bottom right: Brigadier General John T. Croxton, shown here as a colonel, led a detached brigade of 1,100 Federal troopers on a raid over to Tuscaloosa, Alabama. He had instructions to burn anything of military value, including the University of Alabama. Wilson was so confident of his numerical and tactical superiority over Forrest's worn-out troopers that he divided his command.

Union General James Harrison Wilson, West Point, 1860, one of the "boy generals" of the Civil War, did not serve in the cavalry branch until February 1864. Then, at the beginning of the Richmond campaign, General Grant assigned him to command a division of Sheridan's cavalry. Wilson managed his assignment with consummate aggressiveness and skill that did not go unnoticed, and he was promoted to chief of cavalry of Sherman's Military Division of the Mississippi in the western theater.

Wilson's natural organizational genius was obvious when he forged the cavalry corps in the west into the best-drilled and -equipped mounted force in the army. Wilson also coped admirably with Kilpatrick when the latter was fired by Meade from the Army of the Potomac.

On March 22, 1865, Brigadier General Wilson led three divisions of cavalry, the largest Federal mounted force heretofore, some 14,000 men, against Selma, Alabama, one of the few remaining industrial centers in the South. The only real Confederate opposition was the legendary Lieutenant General Nathan Bedford Forrest, commanding the cavalry in the Department of Alabama, Mississippi and East Louisiana. Forrest's tired troopers were mounted on worn-out horses, a mere shadow of the effective force they had once been.

Wilson started from Waterloo on the Tennessee River, very near Eastport, and headed southeast to Jasper, across the Black Warrior River to Elyton, meeting little opposition. He turned due south, paralleling the Cahaba River to Montevallo where, on March 31, Forrest tried to stop the Yankee raiders with some cavalry and local Alabama troops, only to be brushed aside. If that were not enough, Wilson captured one of Forrest's couriers carrying plans for Forrest's defensive operations. This knowledge enabled Wilson to send General Edward M. McCook to hold the bridge at Centreville and deny Forrest the use of 3,000 of his men west of the Cahaba River.

Forrest made one final attempt to stop Wilson's force at Bogler's Creek near Ebenezer Church, but was flanked by troopers under Generals Eli Long and Emory Upton. Forrest

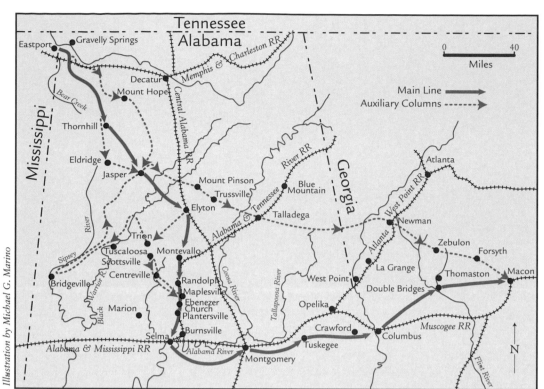

Illustration by Michael G. Marino

Below: Remnants of Kautz's Cavalry Division, serving with the Army of the James, originally 3,300 strong before they ran into Confederates under Major General Wade Hampton at Reams' Station, straggle back to Federal positions. The Federal raiders lost all their wagons and artillery and left their wounded behind. General Wilson gained valuable experience, but Kautz was reassigned to subordinate infantry commands.

Bottom: The Model 1860 Spencer was the most efficient carbine used by Federal cavalry during the war. Sufficient numbers reached units in the field by early 1864 and this advanced weaponry gave Union cavalry a decided tactical advantage. Most of Wilson's men had the seven-shot, magazine-fed breechloader during the raid and the firepower was devastating to Forrest's outnumbered and outgunned units.

was forced to retreat eighteen miles to the Selma defenses. Wilson just overwhelmed Forrest at every turn and captured Selma late in the afternoon of April 2, bagging about 2,700 prisoners. Forrest fought his way out, killing his thirtieth man in personal combat, but the beaten Confederate forces were scattered. Wilson turned east, sweeping away all Southern forces in his path and continuing the greatest independent cavalry mission of the war. Wilson's forces arrived in Macon, Georgia, several weeks later, where hostilities terminated.

Elements of Wilson's cavalry, the 1st Wisconsin and 4th Michigan, participated in the pursuit and capture of Confederate President Jefferson Davis and what remained of the presidential party. Wilson's troopers also captured Vice President Alexander Stephens and Captain Henry Wirz, the Commandant of Andersonville Prison.

Wilson was promoted to the rank of major general on June 21, 1865, in recognition of his service, but the Cavalry Corps was formally dissolved shortly thereafter. With the army reorganization of 1866 he reverted to the rank of lieutenant colonel and served with the Corps of Engineers until he resigned in 1870. He returned to the service as a major general of volunteers during the war with Spain in 1898, and fought in the Boxer Rebellion in China in 1901. Today, even in the light of his distinguished career, he is the least recognized of the great cavalry leaders of the Civil War.

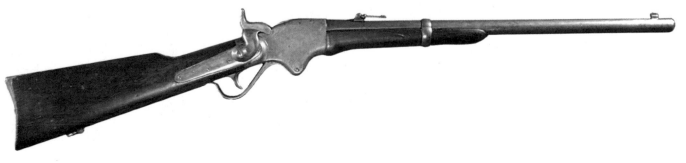

JEB Stuart's Heroic Ride

Right: Major General William Henry Fitzhugh Lee, a son of General Robert E. Lee, was called "Rooney" to avoid confusing him with his cousin, General Fitzhugh Lee. As a colonel, he led the 9th Virginia Cavalry, one of the units that made the armed reconnaissance around the Union army on the Peninsula. He was wounded at Brandy Station, captured at one point and then exchanged, and served until the surrender at Appomattox.

During the Peninsula Campaign of 1862, Federal forces were entrenched before Richmond, along the Chickahominy River, confronting Confederate forces defending the city. In early June, anticipating General Lee's need of timely intelligence regarding Federal positions, Brigadier General J. E. B. Stuart, the new chief of cavalry, sent John Singleton Mosby, then a volunteer scout on Stuart's staff, into the Totopotomoy area to gather information. Mosby discovered only scattered Federal cavalry videttes in the vicinity. The right flank of the Union Army, not anchored and unprotected, was "up in the air" and the critical Union supply line was virtually unguarded and vulnerable to attack.

Stuart communicated this information to General Lee and Lee quickly issued marching orders to his cavalry commander. He told Stuart to "make a scout movement to the rear of the enemy now posted on the Chickahominy,

Right: James Ewell Brown "Jeb" Stuart was the most renowned Confederate cavalryman of the war. He had served as General Lee's aide at Harpers Ferry when John Brown was captured, and by mid-1862 already was a trusted confidant of the general. When Lee wanted to know the disposition of McClellan's army, he assigned the reconnaissance to Stuart with full confidence.

with a view of gaining intelligence of his operations, communications, etc." Stuart was to take only supplies he could carry, "destroy his wagons and not to hazard unnecessarily your command." Lee needed confirmation that McClellan's right flank and supply line was indeed the Achilles heel of the Union forces.

Stuart chose his best men. These were Colonel Fitzhugh Lee, 1st Virginia Cavalry, and Colonel W. H. F. "Rooney" Lee, 9th Virginia Cavalry, who commanded elements of their respective regiments and eight companies attached from the 4th Virginia Cavalry. Lieutenant Colonel Jeff Martin led the Mississippians of the Jeff Davis Legion. A section of Stuart's horse artillery, a 12-pounder howitzer and a small English Blakely rifle, were under the command of Lieutenant James Breathed. Altogether Stuart's force mounted about 1,200 men.

At 2:00 AM, June 12, on the beginning of this great adventure, Stuart's troopers swung into the saddle and headed north up the Brook Turnpike that ran out of Richmond toward

Louisa Court House (Stuart's command was gathered along the Richmond & Fredericksburg RR just north of Richmond). Stuart diverted the route of march to the northwest for several miles to confuse any observers before resuming the march north to the South Anna River. There he turned due east and bivouacked on the Winston farm near Hanover Court House after a twenty-two-mile march. Before dawn, Friday the 13th, Stuart's

cavalrymen were quietly back in the saddle, continuing east toward Hanover Court House, with the 9th Virginia Cavalry in the van.

When the Confederates reached this first objective they found 150 regulars of the 6th U.S. Cavalry blocking their way. Stuart sent Fitz Lee and his 1st Virginia Cavalry to flank the Federals, and then charged with his remaining force. Fitz Lee was slowed by a swampy area and failed to contain the Federal riders, who scampered off toward Mechanicsville.

The column reformed with the 9th Virginia in the lead, and with scouts under the command of Lieutenant W. T. Robins probing the route ahead of the main body. As Robins' riders approached the Totopotomoy they found the narrow bridge intact and with Federal pickets on their side of the creek. The Federals stampeded for the bridge at the sight of the Confederates, but the structure was so narrow that it caused a bottleneck that allowed the Confederates to capture a number of the fleeing Yankees. The rest of the 9th Virginia came up and elements under Captain William Latane galloped up a hill to assault troopers of the 5th U.S. Cavalry that had regrouped after the precipitous withdrawal.

The two groups of cavalry collided in hand-to-hand combat. In the general melee of the fight at Haw's Shop, legend has it that Captain Latane charged Captain W. B. Royall, the commander of the Union contingent, and severely wounded him with his saber. Royall drew his revolver and shot Latane dead as the

Left: **Virginia cavalryman sketched early in the war carrying an obsolescent Hall Carbine. Artist and soldier Allen Christian Redwood (1844-1922) served in the 55th Virginia and drew on his wartime experiences for subject matter in his post-war career. Stuart's troopers would have appeared much as this cavalryman with all his equipment.**

Below left: **Confederate mounted units used various patterns of saddles but tried to achieve some modicum of standardization. The McClellan saddle was the most popular and also regarded as the most comfortable for the horse. This saddle is a brass-trimmed Confederate copy of the Federal McClellan, probably made in the eastern theater. It is fitted with patent breakaway stirrups.**

Below: **Route of Stuart's cavalry around McClellan's whole army.**

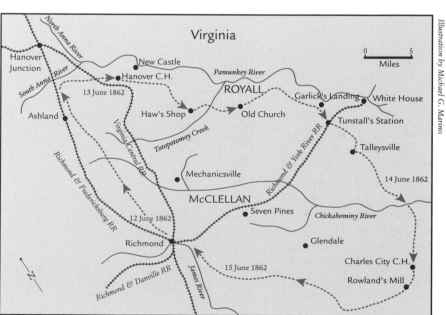

Illustration by Michael G. Marino

ginia drove the troopers of the 5th U.S. Cavalry from their bivouac and proceeded to plunder the camp. Here, Stuart made the momentous decision to continue east to Tunstall's Station to strike McClellan's supply line, just nine miles ahead, rather than return to Hanover Court House and face Federal units assembling there.

The pursuing Federal cavalry were under the command of Brigadier General Philip St. George Cooke. A Virginian by birth, Cooke was Stuart's father-in-law. Even though he wasn't on the field during the raid, the embarrassment suffered by Union mounted forces insured that General Cooke never saw field service again. Estimates of the size of Stuart's force were greatly inflated by the Federals. Elements of the already bloodied 5th and 6th U.S. Cavalry, the 5th Pennsylvania Cavalry and a brigade of slow marching infantry commanded by Colonel Gouverneur K. Warren appeared in no hurry to catch up with them.

The advance party of 9th Virginia under Lieutenant Robins led the way into Tunstall's Station. The Federals were caught by surprise by the screaming gray troopers, and a number immediately surrendered. Although sorely tempted by the proximity of the huge supply depot at White House, Stuart realized that there was much to do at Tunstall's. When the Confederates rode out they left thirty acres of burning wagons full of Federal supplies.

The 9th Virginia led the way through Talleyville in the dark. They surprised some Union sutlers' wagons chock full of figs, candy, canned meats, lemons, cakes – all unavailable to Southern forces – that they plundered with wild abandon. Mosby described it as "a carnival of fun."

Dawn found the raiders stopped at the flooded Chickahominy. Stuart's men managed

Above: Stuart and his fast-moving riders overran the camp of the 5th U.S. Cavalry near Old Church. Such a camp may have appeared similar to this image of carefully aligned, pitched tents with parade ground but not as elaborate. Some of the men of this Federal unit had served with Stuart in the old army before the war and recognized him.

Right: Brigadier General Philip St. George Cooke faced the family tragedy not uncommon in the Civil War. He commanded the cavalry units facing his son-in-law, "Jeb" Stuart, during Stuart's first big ride. General Cooke was spared the anguish of actually fighting his son-in-law as he was away in Washington, and he saw no further field service during the war. His son, General John Rogers Cooke, commanded an infantry brigade in the Army of Northern Virginia and two of his daughters were married to Confederate officers.

Far right: These veteran troopers are men of the 5th U.S. Regular Cavalry that served as General Grant's bodyguard in the closing campaign of the war. Soldiers in the regular army, not volunteers, some of these same men faced Rooney Lee's men in several confrontations along the Pamunky River during Stuart's ride in June 1862.

Union troopers broke. Four Confederate enlisted men were wounded during the engagement. Five Federal soldiers were killed and many were wounded but escaped. A number of prisoners were captured. The body of Captain Latane was taken to the nearby Brockenbrough home and buried in the yard by the women, children and slaves of the place.

The march commenced again toward Old Church, this time with Fitz Lee's 1st Virginia Cavalry in the lead. At Old Church, the 1st Vir-

to build a shaky footbridge across the torrent and swam their horses across, expecting to be overrun by pursuing Yankees. The artillery pieces were pulled across practically under water. It took over three anxious hours for Stuart's command to cross the river and get back on the road to Charles City Court House. They were still in enemy territory, thirty-five long miles from safety.

Stuart turned command of the column over to Fitz Lee and began the last dash to bring the news that McClellan's flank was indeed "in the air." After resting his men, Fitz Lee started the exhausted column toward Richmond around 11:00 PM. The ride was quiet; most of the troopers were asleep in the saddle.

In three days, Stuart covered 150 miles, through Hanover, New Kent, Charles City, and Henrico Counties, captured scores of Yankee prisoners, and brought General Lee the information he needed. The result was Lee's victory during the Seven Days Battles and McClellan's withdrawal from the Peninsula.

The loss of Captain Latane captured the imagination of the South and became the subject of a painting, *The Burial of Latane*, by William De Hartburn Washington, done in

1864. Subsequently, John Ruben Thompson wrote a poem describing the burial; it became immensely popular. In 1868, A. G. Campbell produced an engraving done after the painting, copies of which hung for years in most parlors in homes in the South. The original Washington painting is now in the collections of the Museum of the Confederacy in Richmond, Virginia.

Above: The Chickahominy River as a topographical feature played a primary role in many of the battles around Richmond. Stuart and his raiders crossed the small river on their initial feint north, searching for the exposed right flank of the Federal army. Lieutenant John S. Mosby with several other riders had already scouted the route in advance.

Below: Stuart and his subordinates were honing their skills on this first major raid. The raid was primarily an intelligence gathering operation but later forays would be aimed at critical supply lines. These developing skills included the destruction of the Union supply system, and this derailed military train was the result of a visit by Confederate raiders.

Morgan: Thunderbolt of the Confederacy

Below left: **Brigadier General John Hunt Morgan was the nemesis of Federal troops in Kentucky, Tennessee, Indiana and Ohio. His relentless forays into his home state of Kentucky kept the divided loyalties of that area in constant upheaval, but recruiting efforts were not as successful as expected.**

Below center: **Major General Edmund Kirby Smith led part of General Braxton Bragg's penetration into Kentucky in August 1862. After the indecisive battle at Perryville, Morgan joined Smith during the withdrawal. Smith authorized Morgan's raid into Lexington and Versailles and his assaults on General Buell's supply lines facilitated the Confederate withdrawal.**

Below right: **Major General William Starke Rosecrans replaced General Don Carlos Buell after the latter's utter failure in Kentucky, and the Union command was designated the Army of the Cumberland. Morgan pillaged Rosecrans' lines of supply and communications with the same ease as when he operated against Buell.**

Confederate Generals Braxton Bragg and E. Kirby Smith had invaded Kentucky in two columns in August 1862 and were successful in their operations into late September. There was still hope that substantial numbers of Kentuckians would rally to the Confederate cause. Union forces under Major General Don Carlos Buell moved out from Louisville to confront the Southern forces. Elements of the two opposing armies met at Perryville on October 8. Unusually hot weather and lack of water plagued both sides. Federal forces were pushed back after a hard, day-long fight, but Confederate troops involved suffered nearly 25 percent casualties. This battle ended the Southern incursion into the border state.

Confederate Colonel John Hunt Morgan's Kentucky Cavalry joined Lieutenant General E. Kirby Smith's forces during the withdrawal. While encamped about twenty-five miles south of Richmond, Kentucky, the scene of a previous Rebel victory at the end of August, Morgan proposed to General Smith that he take his 1,800 Kentuckians and raid behind Union lines, destroying rail and supply routes to distract the already painfully slow Union

pursuit. Kirby Smith concurred, and Morgan led Lieutenant Colonel Basil W. Duke, 2nd Kentucky Cavalry, Colonel Richard Gano, 3rd Kentucky Cavalry, and Major William C. Breckinridge with a battalion of Kentucky cavalry, northwest to Lexington, where with little effort the force captured the garrison of the lightly defended town on October 18. Morgan's party then headed west to Versailles.

For the next twelve days Morgan and his men encountered little opposition as they swung through Lawrenceburg, Bloomfield, Bardstown, Elizabethville, and Litchfield. They crossed the Green River between Woodbury and Morgantown, and then the Muddy River south of Rochester, and continued toward Greenville and reached Hopkinsville on October 25. Morgan's men spent three idyllic days enjoying rest and relaxation with the sympathetic population that wined and dined the tired Confederates, the high point of the raid. The Confederates reached Springfield, Tennessee, on November 1 and later went on to Gallatin. A few Union captives were paroled along the route, and some small bridges were destroyed, but Morgan's troopers suffered but few casualties.

The Union General Buell was sacked because of lackluster performance against the Confederates in Kentucky, and he was replaced by Major General William Starke Rosecrans. Although the Confederate riders were little more than a nuisance on this raid, the foray increased the already existing anxiety of Union forces in the area, and did precipitate the Union command change.

The Christmas Raid, December 21, 1862–January 2, 1863

A month and a half later, General Bragg ordered newly married and recently promoted Brigadier General Morgan back into Kentucky to cut the Louisville & Nashville Railroad, the extended and exposed supply route of Union forces under the command of Major General Rosecrans, the new area commander. Morgan mustered his riders at Alexandria, Tennessee, on December 21, 1862. His force consisted of two brigades, about 3,100 riders, well armed mostly with English Enfield rifles. Lieutenant Colonel Basil W. Duke commanded the 2nd, 3rd and 8th Kentucky Cavalry, supported by Palmer's Battery. Colonel William Breckinridge led the 9th, 10th, 11th and 14th Kentucky Cavalry, supported by White's and Corbett's Batteries. The mission was the destruction of two huge trestles of the Louisville & Nashville Railroad at Muldraugh's Hill, near Elizabethtown, Kentucky.

The Kentucky cavalry rode out at 9:00 AM on the morning of December 22 and crossed the Cumberland River. At Glasgow the next day they had a sharp fight with a Michigan

cavalry unit that fled up the Louisville Pike, and then the Confederates camped before Elizabethtown. The Federal garrison there consisted of 600 bluecoats of the 91st Illinois Infantry commanded by Lieutenant Colonel Harry S. Smith. After fruitless negotiations, Morgan promptly shelled the town with a 10-pounder Parrott Rifle and several small bronze mountain howitzers, affectionately referred to by the Rebels as "Morgan's Bull Pups." Soon a white flag was observed above one of the Federal positions, reportedly a pair of lady's bloomers, and the Yanks surrendered, to the chagrin of their colonel who was later found safe in a cellar.

Realizing that Federal units were rapidly closing in, and with the mission having been accomplished, Morgan wisely led his force back to the Cumberland River and crossed it to safety on January 2, 1863. During the adventure they destroyed the two big trestles – which, being more than 500 feet in length and over 50 feet high, made a great fire – a number of smaller bridges and three depots. Long stretches of the L & N track and $2,000,000 in supplies and equipment were also destroyed. Morgan lost two men killed, 24 wounded and 64 missing while taking 1,800 Federal prisoners and inflicting substantial casualties on Union forces.

Above: Marauding Confederate raiders like John Hunt Morgan forced Federal authorities to go to considerable efforts to protect lines of communication and supply with elaborate fortifications. This heavily fortified bridge across the Cumberland River at Nashville is complete with defensive cupolas and double gates that could be closed to deny use of the bridge.

Below left: General Morgan with his wife. Mrs. Morgan was the exemplification of a Southern belle and devoted to her husband. After his extraordinary escape from the Ohio State Penitentiary, Morgan assumed command of the Department of Southwestern Virginia. He was killed by Federal forces on September 4, 1864, in Greenville, Tennessee.

Left: Federal railroad repair crews worked almost around the clock to keep up with Morgan's efforts. This crew replaces ties, relays rail, and wonders where they will be doing the same work the next day. It was impossible for Federal troops to guard every yard of track and every bridge site, while Morgan's mobility allowed his raiders to strike almost at will.

Indiana and Ohio Raid, July 2-26, 1863

General Braxton Bragg's forces were based at Tullahoma, Tennessee, during mid-summer 1863. Bragg, fearful of offensive action by Federals under Rosecrans and Burnside, decided to withdraw to defenses around Chattanooga. He ordered General Morgan to cover this retrograde movement, but to confine his operations to that area south of the Ohio River. Morgan's mission was to harass Rosecrans and threaten Louisville.

Morgan had already led several successful raids, and possibly had become overconfident. The general had two brigades commanded by Colonels Duke and Adam R. Johnson, 2,460 riders in all, supported by two 10-pounder Parrott Rifles and two 12-pounder howitzers. They left Burkesville, Kentucky, on July 2 and crossed the Cumberland River, even though Federal Generals George L. Hartsuff and Henry M. Judah and their 10,000 men were guarding the river. Two days later, north of Columbia, Morgan's men were bloodied when

they fought the 25th Michigan Infantry under Colonel Orlando H. Moore at Tabb's Bend, near the Green River Bridge. On July 5 Morgan's band captured the 300-man garrison at Lebanon. One of the casualties of the engagement was the general's younger brother, Lieutenant Tom Morgan. The raiders proceeded by Springfield to Bardstown, where they wrecked the tracks of the L & N, and then approached Brandenburg on the Ohio River.

There, in direct disobedience of Bragg's orders, on the morning of July 9 Morgan took his command across the Ohio River on two captured steamboats. He was fired on by some Indiana militia with a field piece, but easily made the crossing and was into Indiana by midnight. Union pursuit had been building since the beginning of the raid, and Brigadier General Edward H. Hobson, leading the advance party of General Judah's command, was only hours behind Morgan.

This raid had by now stirred up a hornet's nest. Both Indiana and Ohio had called out every available militia unit and Morgan was forced to evade or engage at every crossroad.

Below left: Morgan's Raiders were a proud and independent lot. The image of George W. Bowman, 2nd Kentucky Cavalry, with serious face but jauntily tilted wide-brimmed hat, conveys an aura of resolute professionalism. Part "devil may care" and part "deadly serious," this man is a veteran.

Below right: Many of Morgan's men were captured during the raid into Ohio and Indiana and were sent to the Federal stockade at Camp Douglas, south of Chicago. George Bowman was one of these unfortunate men, shown seated, center, with four other Confederate soldiers. All appear to be well uniformed with nine-button shell jackets and vests.

Below center: Federal Major C. P. Wilson carried this .44 caliber Remington New Model Army Revolver. Major Wilson captured George Bowman during Morgan's Indiana-Ohio raid. Wilson's name is engraved on the butt strap of the revolver.

Bottom left: It was not unusual for Federal buttons to be used on Confederate uniforms, particularly when there was an abundant supply from captured Union supplies. These Federal eagle buttons are from a coat worn by George W. Bowman during his service in Morgan's cavalry.

Far right: Unit insignia or distinctive devices were not authorized in Confederate forces and their use was very limited. Surviving examples are rare. This extraordinary jeweler-made and -engraved silver pin in the form of a crescent over a star bears the initials of George W. Bowman on the crescent, and the unit designation, 2nd Ky Cav., on the star.

The Confederates were often in the saddle for twenty-one hours a day. Throughout the raid Morgan made ingenious use of the talents of George Ellsworth, his traveling telegrapher. Ellsworth repeatedly tapped into Union lines to transmit false and misleading reports, confounding pursuing Federal forces.

The bold Kentuckian's route of march took the raiding party through Corydon, north to Salem, and then over to Vienna, and then northeast through Sunman and Hamilton. Here, Morgan turned back south and penetrated the suburbs of Cincinnati during a night march, before again turning east toward Williamsburg and Jasper. This was the longest continuous march of

Far left: Many of the Kentucky cavalrymen captured on the Indiana and Ohio raid were sent to Camp Douglas in Illinois. This image shows Confederate prisoners of war on parade at that camp. The men were quartered in the one-story barracks in the background.

Left: The divided loyalties of Kentucky were among the numerous tragedies of the Civil War. Edward Henry Hobson was another Kentuckian loyal to the Union and he raised the 13th Kentucky (Union) Infantry Regiment. General Hobson assisted in the capture of John Hunt Morgan at Buffington's Island, Ohio, and, later in the war in a role reversal, Morgan captured him.

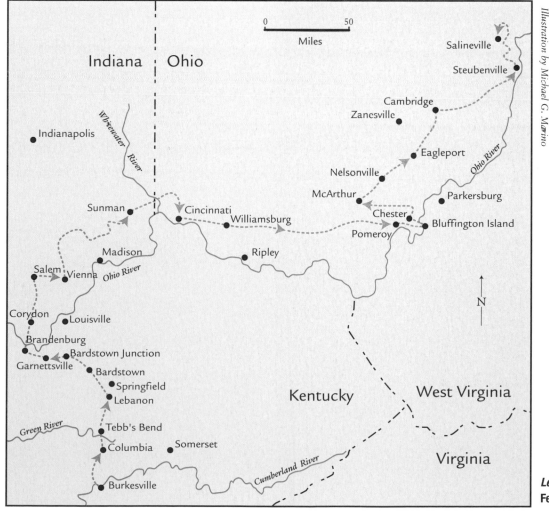

Illustration by Michael G. Marino

Left: Morgan's ill-fated ride into Federal captivity.

Below: Depots and rolling stock were inviting targets for mobile marauders. The ease of destruction of such strategic material was a constant nightmare for Union commanders. Thousands of troops that were desperately needed to prosecute the war were bled from front line combat units to provide necessary rear area security for sites like this rail yard with Union cavalry in the distance.

the war, covering an astounding ninety miles in thirty-five hours, skirmishing along the way.

But Morgan's luck ran out on the morning of July 19 at Buffington's Island in the Ohio River, on the Ohio-West Virginia state line. Union forces descended on the fleeing Confederates from all directions, supported by a Union gunboat, USS *Moose*, on the river. General Hobson's troops killed or wounded nearly 120 of the raiders and captured 700 of them, including Colonel Duke.

Hobson's men pursued the remaining Confederates relentlessly for six more days, finally capturing General Morgan, his brother, Dick, and 364 officers and men near Beaver Creek, Ohio, close to the Pennsylvania state line, on July 26. The raiders were confined at the Ohio State Penitentiary in Columbus as common

criminals rather than as prisoners of war. Morgan and several other men tunneled out and escaped during the night of November 23, 1863.

Ironically, Morgan captured Hobson and his whole command near Cynthiana, Kentucky, in June 1864. General Morgan was later killed in action at Greenville, Tennessee, September 3, 1864.

The raid effectively accomplished the mission and terrorized the local population of Ohio and Indiana. Morgan captured and paroled 6,000 Federal soldiers during the rampage. Some 14,000 Union regular troops had to be detailed from other duties to contend with the marauding Kentuckians and 120,000 emergency militia were called to duty in two states. Morgan's men occupied fifty-two towns, destroyed thirty-four bridges, tore up track all over the area, and damaged hundreds of thousands of dollars' worth of public and private property. The adventure also made history as being the longest cavalry raid of the war, with Morgan and his men traveling 700 miles in twenty-five days of almost constant combat against Federal and local state militia units. But it ended in a disastrous defeat.

Nevertheless, this wild ride and his miraculous escape insured General Morgan a place high on the list of Confederate legends. Today, a magnificent equestrian statue of General Morgan in Lexington, Kentucky, is just one of the numerous reminders of his incredible career. His sobriquet, "Thunderbolt of the Confederacy," aptly describes the dashing and daring character of John Hunt Morgan.

Right: James Murrell Shackelford raised the 8th Kentucky (Union) Cavalry and was colonel of the regiment. Promoted brigadier general, he commanded the 1st Brigade, 2nd Division, XXIII Corps, and was instrumental in chasing Morgan to ground in Ohio. Morgan actually surrendered to the Union Kentuckian after the long pursuit.

Far right: Colonel Richard C. "Dick" Morgan rode with General John Hunt Morgan, his brother, during the raid into Indiana and Ohio. Both officers were captured and Colonel Morgan was eventually sent to Fort Delaware, a prison outside of Wilmington, Delaware.

Above: General Edward H. Hobson and Federal units under his command captured General Morgan and some of his raiders at Buffington's Island, Ohio, in July 1863. This newspaper illustration, produced from a sketch by Henry Lovie, depicts the action at Licking Creek Bridge near Cynthiana, Kentucky, in June 1864, where Morgan turned the tables and captured General Hobson.

Left: This carte-de-visite is a bust portrait of General Morgan. His sisters were married to Colonel, later General, Basil W. Duke, 2nd Kentucky Cavalry, who served under Morgan and took over command of the Kentucky Cavaliers after his death, and Major General A. P. Hill who commanded the 3rd Corps in the Army of Northern Virginia.

Van Dorn's Raid on Holly Springs

Below: **Major General Earl Van Dorn, after early service in Virginia, was placed in charge of the Army of the West in the Trans-Mississippi theater in January 1862. His performance in the battles at Pea Ridge, Arkansas, and later at Corinth against Federal General William S. Rosecrans was less than spectacular and he was given command of cavalry in the Army of Mississippi under General John C. Pemberton.**

During the winter of 1862, General Ulysses S. Grant planned a campaign to capture Vicksburg, open the Mississippi River Valley, and cut the Confederacy in two. Using the Mississippi Central Railroad, Grant built an enormous ordnance and supply depot at Holly Springs, Mississippi, to support this operation.

Confederate forces in Mississippi were inadequate to stop the Federal juggernaut in a pitched battle. Lieutenant Colonel John C. Griffith, a Texas cavalryman, developed the concept of destroying the Union supply depot behind Grant's advancing forces, thereby depriving him of food and ammunition with which to press his campaign. On December 5 Griffith forwarded this idea to Major General John C. Pemberton, commanding forces in the area. In short order the idea was approved and Pemberton placed Brigadier General Earl Van Dorn in command on December 12.

Earl Van Dorn, one of the South's most respected generals at the beginning of the war, had by no means lived up to expectations, and he was removed from army command after his poor performance at Pea Ridge, Arkansas, and Corinth, Mississippi. Nevertheless, Pemberton placed him in command of a cobbled-together cavalry division made up of units he had never seen nor commanded. As fate would have it, the small independent command was ideally tailored to his military aptitude and capabilities.

The division consisted of three brigades. The Texas Brigade included the 3rd, 6th, 9th, and 27th Texas Cavalry commanded by Griffith. The Tennessee Brigade, commanded by Colonel William H. Jackson, included the 7th Tennessee Cavalry, while the Missouri Brigade under Colonel Robert "Red Bob" McCulloch included the 2nd Missouri Cavalry and elements of several other Missouri units, and the 1st Mississippi Cavalry under Colonel Robert A. Pinson – a total of 3,500 poorly armed and mounted troopers.

On December 15 the strike force was stealthily mustered near Grenada, Mississippi. Each of the men was issued three days' rations, sixty rounds of ammunition, a box of matches and a bottle of turpentine. At 2:30 AM the next morning, they moved out in a cold, steady rain. The riders crossed the Yalobusha River at Graysport and continued northeast toward Houston, slowed by bottomless roads caused by the continuous rain. They passed through Houston and just missed a chance encounter with Federal cavalry at Pontotoc. On the night

Left: The Mississippi Central Railroad connected the large Federal depot at LaGrange, Tennessee, with Grant's headquarters then at Grenada, Mississippi. The Federals developed a substantial advance supply depot at Holly Springs, conveniently on the railroad to supply Grant's whole force as he moved against the Confederate citadel at Vicksburg. The rail depot was overflowing with supplies when Van Dorn's raiders overran the town.

Left: The armory in Holly Springs was a small facility and only altered and refurbished arms for Confederate forces early in the war. When Federal forces occupied the town the buildings were utilized as a hospital complex. Most of the buildings were burned, either accidentally on or purpose, during the hours that Van Dorn held the town. Large quantities of captured alcohol probably played some part in the fires.

of December 18 the men bivouacked north of the Tallahatchie, above New Albany, and then rode north the following day toward Ripley, turning west on a little-used, overgrown lane toward Holly Springs. They stopped about fifteen miles from their objective. The excited cavalrymen spent a shivering night without fires waiting for dawn, checking arms and equipment, and going over assault plans.

At first light, on December 20, the Confederates, in two columns in ranks of fours, thundered into town and overran the just-waking Federal infantry, who scattered in their nightclothes. The Union garrison of slightly more than 1,500 men under the command of Colonel Robert C. Murphy was billeted at three dispersed locations. The luckless soldiers of elements of the 20th, 26th, 29th, 62nd and 101st Illinois Infantry were caught totally by surprise and most just surrendered. Colonel Murphy appeared in his nightshirt, while Colonel Charles Fox, the provost marshal, was captured in bed with his wife. One element was on the square around the Court House,

another at the Railroad Depot; six companies of the 2nd Illinois Cavalry were at the Fairgrounds, north of town.

Company G, the "Noxubee County Cowboys," 1st Mississippi Cavalry, led the Confederate units that hit the cavalry encampment. The blue troopers were saddled and mounted and tried to make of fight of it, but were overwhelmed. Major J. J. Mudd and about seventy Illinois troopers managed to escape to Memphis. The action was over almost before it began, and there were few casualties on either side. Almost the whole garrison of Yanks was paroled in a matter of hours.

One resident described the Southerners as the "most disreputable looking fellows." They wore ragged uniforms worn off to the knee; some were without coats and shoes, and their mounts looked like skeletons. From 8:00 AM until 4:00 PM these men brought all captured supplies and equipment into the street and burned them. This conflagration included at least 1,000 wagons and 2,000 bales of cotton. One witness said so much sutlers' whiskey was

Above: Elements of Van Dorn's force charged up the road in front of the courthouse and into the town square in their initial assault. Union soldiers of several regiments quickly surrendered in this location. Ordnance stores warehoused around the square were brought into the streets for destruction, but through negligence or drunkenness the fires got out of hand and a major conflagration occurred, with the loss of a number of buildings.

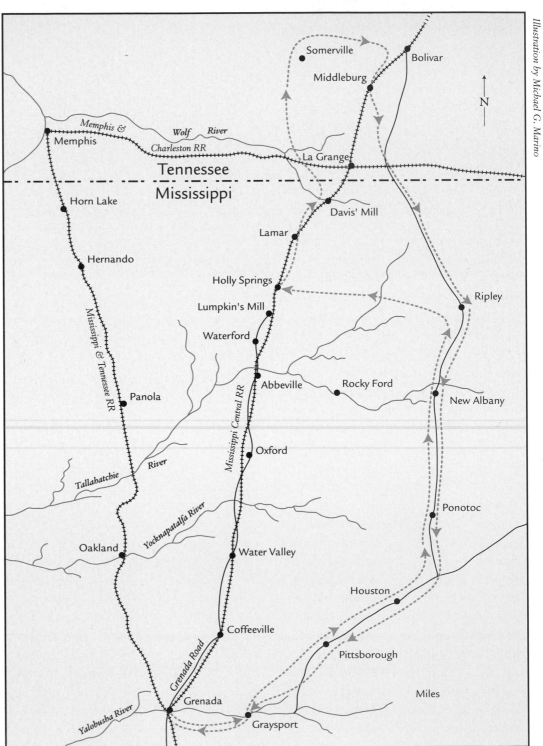

Right: Line of march of Van Dorn's raiders to Grant's supply depot at Holly Springs.

Left: This St. Andrews Cross silk battle-flag was carried by General Earl Van Dorn's escort and was the headquarters' designating color. Western army Confederate formations subsequently adopted several other pattern flags, rectangular in shape rather than square like this early example.

poured out that it ran like a river through the street. Other accounts indicate that much liquor was drunk by both Confederate and paroled Union soldiers before any was dumped.

Be that as it may, the fire got out of control and most of the buildings on the north and east sides of the square were destroyed. The Masonic Temple was used for ordnance storage, and when the fire reached it the detonation was reported as spectacular. The whole building seemed to rise into the air before it "just disintegrated." Even the new hospital went up in smoke. A Union paymaster was captured along with a large amount of Federal banknotes, some of it in uncut sheets. Local lore says the origin of several present-day family inheritances can be traced to this "lost Yankee money."

When the "disreputable fellows" rode out, their horses staggered under the load. Each man had a new blue (Yankee) uniform, between two and six new Colt revolvers, one or two new Sharps carbines, blankets, rubber ground cloths, boots and hats, and whatever else they could carry.

The Confederates left town going north on the old Hudsonville Road toward Sylvestria Church. The next day Union cavalry forces re-occupied the smoldering town, but by then Van Dorn's fast-moving riders were near Davis' Mill on the Wolf River, near the Tennessee line. Van Dorn threatened the strong garrison at Bolivar and then headed south back toward Ripley.

General Grant was apoplectic when he heard the news, and ordered Federal cavalry to chase Van Dorn into Tennessee if necessary. After a series of lost couriers and false starts the Federals began the pursuit. Federal Colonel Grierson and

his units were hours behind Van Dorn, and when they finally caught up with them near Ripley subordinates refused to launch a night assault, and the frustrating pursuit ended at Pontotoc. Van Dorn and his men triumphantly arrived back at Grenada at the end of the year.

The raid on Holly Springs was a resounding success tactically and strategically. Van Dorn covered nearly 400 miles in two weeks, inflicting casualties to Union forces in excess of his total force, and destroying 1,500,000 dollars' worth of supplies. Grant was forced to give up the initiative, withdraw to Memphis and postpone his Vicksburg Campaign because of shortages caused by the raid. It was a great boost to sagging Southern morale to see Federal troops run out of northern Mississippi, if only for a short time. Colonel Murphy became the sacrificial lamb of the affair and was dismissed from the service "for his cowardly and disgraceful conduct at Holly Springs."

Earl Van Dorn was shot and killed several months after his moment of glory by a Dr. Peters, husband of the lovely Jessie Peters, with whom the general evidently had been too familiar. She reportedly gave birth to a baby girl eight and one half months after the general's unexpected demise. Dr. and Mrs. Peters divorced but subsequently remarried.

General Grant captured Vicksburg on July 4, 1863, but Earl Van Dorn's audacity had stalled the Union advance by at least three months.

Left: Van Dorn found his niche as an independent cavalry commander. His operation against Grant's supply base at Holly Springs was a textbook success and delayed Grant's investment of Vicksburg for several months. Van Dorn had a wandering eye for the ladies and his unfortunate demise at the hands of a jealous husband cut short his career.

Mosby – The Gray Ghost

Below: Colonel John Singleton Mosby, clean-shaven and boyish, posing with some of his officers and men. Most of the men, some no more than boys, appear even younger. None wears a military hat, and the colonel has placed a plume in his hatband. Federal commanders stationed in northern Virginia already feared Mosby and his men by the time this photograph was taken.

Colonel Sir Percy Wyndham, a supercilious and arrogant English soldier of fortune, commanded a Federal brigade of cavalry billeted near Fairfax Court House, Virginia, just south of Washington. Flamboyant Confederate Captain John Singleton Mosby's operations against Wyndham's troopers, which included harassment of sentries and outposts, and the capture of horses and forage, were a constant source of irritation and embarrassment. Unable to confront the elusive partisan, the frustrated Colonel sent Mosby a petulant message in which he referred to the Confederates as "horse thieves." Captain Mosby graciously responded that all the

stolen horses carried riders who were armed with "sabres, carbines and pistols."

The senior officer at Fairfax was the youngest general in the Federal Army at the time, the arrogant and vain twenty-four-year-old Brigadier General Edwin H. Stoughton. He had chosen the location for his headquarters as a place to have a good time, fifteen miles from Washington and away from supervision by more senior officers. This situation was to be the stage for one of the most publicized and romanticized raids of the Civil War.

One of the newest recruits of Mosby's command was a deserter from the Federal 5th New York Cavalry, Sergeant "Big Yankee" Ames,

who had detailed and intimate knowledge of the picket line patrolled by Wyndham's units and the gaps in it. This windfall of information, added to Mosby's familiarity with every back road and byway of the area, enabled the raiders to formalize a plan to capture both the Union general and colonel in one fell swoop.

On March 9, 1863, at 2:00 AM, Mosby and twenty-nine raiders set out for Fairfax. The night was cold and rainy as the men rode southeast on the Little River Turnpike nearly to the toll gate west of Chantilly, before heading south, going between Centreville and Germantown, and approaching the Court House from the southwest. The few tired, cold sentries assumed that the riders, with their uniforms covered by rain gear, were Federal cavalry returning from routine patrol – until it was too late.

The Federal officers and headquarters personnel had spent the evening drinking champagne in the company of the local ladies, blissfully ignorant of the approaching Confederates. It happened that Colonel Wyndham was called away to Washington City and missed the festivities. By the time Mosby and his men arrived, the party-goers were fast asleep. The Confederates split into assault parties, each with specific objectives. Some searched the town for horses while others went after individuals.

Mosby was disappointed to find Wyndham gone but was informed that Stoughton's residence was nearby. Mosby approached the house, knocked on the door, and announced he was a Federal courier. When the door was eventually opened by one of the general's staff, the officer found a Colt revolver shoved in his face, and he dutifully led the Confederates to the general's bottle-littered bedroom. The most amusing account has Captain Mosby pulling back the bed covers and slapping Stoughton's bare behind. Whatever the actual circumstances, the befuddled young general found himself a prisoner of war.

As planned, the raiding party with their captives gathered at 3:30 AM in the square and rode south out of town. As they galloped away, the retiring riders woke up Lieutenant Colonel Robert Johnstone, 5th New York Cavalry, who surmised something was amiss and abruptly ran out the back of his quarters buck naked and jumped into the outhouse to hide. Lieutenant L. L. O'Conner, Provost

Above left: **The Court House at Fairfax, Virginia, in the heart of Mosby's area of operations. The unfortunate Federal General Stoughton chose to make his headquarters near here...like the hen strolling into the fox's den. His encounter with Mosby effectively ended his military career.**

Above: **Fun-loving Brigadier General Edwin Henry Stoughton was at the wrong place at the wrong time. Lax security around his headquarters allowed Mosby's midnight callers to whisk him away, and the humiliated Federal general soon found himself in the presence of his old friend, General Fitzhugh Lee. After General Stoughton was exchanged he returned to civilian life as an attorney.**

Left: **This full standing view of Colonel Mosby, with painted studio backdrop, portrays him perfectly near the end of the war. Confidence and independence still are obvious from his demeanor. The colonel carried two revolvers with which he was reputed to be very proficient. Mosby did not favor the saber, so the one upon which he leans here may be a studio prop.**

Marshall at Fairfax, reportedly was so drunk that he was unaware of the raid.

The party turned southwest and then west around Centreville and on toward Groveton. During the ride out some of the Federal prisoners managed to slip away. The party went west on the Warrenton Turnpike to Warrenton, where Mosby personally presented General Stoughton to General Fitzhugh Lee, commander of Confederate cavalry in the area.

Northern and Southern newspapers had a field day, but accounts greatly differed. In actuality, Mosby and twenty-nine men infiltrated Union lines to a brigade headquarters, captured one general, two captains, twenty-eight other ranks and more than fifty horses,

without firing a shot. The official report submitted by Lieutenant O'Conner placed the strength of the Confederate forces at 300 men, typical of Union inflated strength assessments when dealing with the "Gray Ghost."

President Lincoln's comment about the affair was more to the point. He said, "Well, I'm sorry to hear about that. I don't care so much about the general. I can make another in five minutes. I do hate to lose the horses." There is no record of any comments by Colonel Wyndham upon his return. Shortly after the action a general order was read throughout the Army of Northern Virginia.

As a direct result of this operation Mosby was promoted to the rank of major and au-

Right: John Mosby appears here as a newly appointed major, promoted by orders of General J. E. B. Stuart. His elevation in rank was due to his brilliant capture of General Stoughton without the loss of a man. Mosby was authorized to recruit a battalion of men, the 43rd Battalion of Virginia Cavalry. So many volunteers flocked to join the unit that dozens had to be turned away.

GENERAL ORDER

CAPTAIN JOHN S. MOSBY has for a long time attracted the attention of his Generals by his boldness, skill and success, so signally displayed in his numerous forays upon the invaders of his native State.

None knew his daring enterprise and dashing heroism better than those foul invaders though strangers themselves to such noble traits.

His late brilliant exploit – the capture of Brigadier General Stoughton, U.S.A., 2 captains, 30 other prisoners, together with their arms, equipments and 58 horses – justifies his recognition in General orders. This feat, almost unparalleled in the war, was performed in the midst of the enemy's troops at Fairfax Court House, without loss or injury.

The gallant band of Captain Mosby share the glory, as they did the danger of this enterprise and are worthy of such a leader.

J. E. B. STUART
MAJOR GENERAL COMMANDING

thorized to raise the 43rd Battalion of Virginia Cavalry. So many volunteers rallied to his call that the unit eventually had eight companies. Mosby rose to the rank of full colonel by the war's end.

Stoughton resigned from the army shortly after he was exchanged, not that he had much choice, and died Christmas Day 1868, in Boston, at the age of thirty.

During the final twenty-eight months of the war Mosby's command incessantly attacked and harassed the Federal Army. The activities of Mosby and his handful of raiders caused the diversion of 30,000 Union troopers from offensive operations.

General Lee cited Mosby in official reports more often than he did any other officer. Colonel Mosby never surrendered but disbanded his unit on April 21, 1865, and returned to a productive legal practice, serving as an attorney in the Department of Justice. Dozens of books have been written about him and his rangers, and he is the only Civil War personality to have a television series based on his exploits. CBS aired thirty-nine episodes of *The Gray Ghost* in 1957-1959 that were reasonably accurate, including one on the capture of General Stoughton. The show remained in syndication for ten years. The neighboring Virginia counties of Loudon and Fauquier are still considered "Mosby's Confederacy" today.

Left: Colonel Mosby has obviously aged in this image that shows him fully bearded with moustache. The rigor and strain of months of hit-and-run guerrilla warfare have had an effect on the man. The effect of his efforts upon his Union adversaries was much greater.

Below: Mosby is still the young beardless fellow in this photograph taken with an unidentified individual. The likeness may have been made at the same sitting as the group photograph showing Mosby with some of his men. By now, his reputation made, he was causing increased anxiety around "Mosby's country." The Federals never knew where the illusive raiders would appear next.

Stuart's Gettysburg Raid

Below: **Major General J. E. B. Stuart was a spirited, jovial individual who was first and foremost a professional soldier. Stuart knew his cavalry was the eyes and ears of the Confederate army. His personal ambition and ego infrequently skewed his perception, and this raid was one of those times. His loss of communication with General Lee while on this raid left his commander without a clue to movements of the Federal army.**

Right: **"Fitz" Lee commanded one of the three cavalry brigades that made this raid under General J. E. B. Stuart. He and Stuart were particularly close. After Stuart was killed Fitz played an even larger role in cavalry operations. He served as Governor of Virginia after the war and was a major general in the U.S. Army during the Spanish-American War in 1898.**

J. E. B. Stuart's Confederate cavalry had just fought the greatly improved Federal cavalry commanded by Major General Alfred Pleasonton at Brandy Station, Virginia, on June 9, 1863. It was the largest cavalry engagement on American soil and there was not a decisive victory for either side. Stuart was surprised and stung by the ferocity of the Federal attack and probably felt he needed another spectacular raid to redeem himself. General Robert E. Lee's impending invasion of Pennsylvania would give the Confederate cavalier such an opportunity.

The plan for Lee's second invasion of the North assigned Confederate cavalry a crucial mission. Stuart's forces had to conceal the movement of elements of the Army of Northern Virginia from the spying eyes of Federal units, while the Confederates abandoned their positions in Virginia and stole a march north through Maryland and Pennsylvania. This movement would position the Southern army to threaten Washington, Baltimore and Philadelphia, and compel the Union's Army of the Potomac to withdraw from war-ravaged Virginia to confront them. Stuart's units would accomplish the mission by denying Federals the Blue Ridge passes and keeping them east of the mountains as the Army of Northern Virginia marched north.

Late on the afternoon of June 23 General Lee gave his cavalry commander vague, discre-

Above: Confederate cavalrymen were armed with a number of different longarms. Some of the best were carbines and rifles captured from Federal troops. Others, like this Pattern 1856 Iron Mounted Short Rifle, were imported from England. This rifle was a .577 caliber and could fire the standard Federal .58 caliber cartridge.

Left: Private D. E. Goodwyn, Company E, 13th Virginia Cavalry, carved his name and unit on the reverse butt stock of this English Short Rifle. The 13th Virginia was part of General "Rooney" Lee's Brigade. Colonel J. R. Chambliss led the brigade on this raid because Lee was recuperating from a wound received at Brandy Station.

tionary written orders directing Stuart to screen the right flank of the army, Lieutenant General Richard S. Ewell's II Corps, but also giving him great latitude to harass the Union Army. While Stuart was given a very specific task, the man-ner of accomplishing the task was almost to-tally discretionary. This was to become a major, and soon to be fatal, command flaw. Stuart, for reasons unknown to this day, misinterpreted, or possibly just disregarded, his orders and cut

Left: Stuart's cavalry passed the same Fairfax Court House in late June 1863 where his friend Mosby had kidnapped General Stoughton earlier in the year. This site, today swallowed up in the suburbs of Washington, D.C., changed hands countless times during the ebb and flow of the war in northern Virginia.

Right: Stuart's men spent considerable time destroying tracks of the Baltimore & Ohio Railroad when their time and efforts might have been better directed elsewhere. But Lee's orders to Stuart told him to harass the Federal army, and installations like this junction at Hanover, Pennsylvania, were hard to bypass when there was no Federal opposition.

Below: Confederate cavalry used equipment available by capture, importation from overseas, and local manufacture. This saddle is a typical eastern theater saddle of local manufacture known as a Confederate Skeleton Jennifer Pattern saddle with brass trim. The skirts have been removed. There is a brown leather carbine socket attached to the girth ring.

loose from Lee's army to carry out yet another independent ride around the Federal Army.

The headquarters of the Stuart's Cavalry was at Rector's Crossroads, between Upperville and Middleburg. Stuart determined to leave the brigades of Brigadier Generals William E. "Grumble" Jones and Beverly Holcombe Robertson to perform the screening mission, and at 1:00 AM on June 25 rode out with three brigades commanded by Generals Wade Hampton and Fitzhugh Lee and Colonel John R. Chambliss, the latter commanding Rooney Lee's men while that officer was recuperating from a wound sustained at Brandy Station. The 2,000 men of the command rode east toward the Bull Run Mountains but were forced to detour some twenty-three miles around unexpected Federal units, much further than anticipated. The next day they reached Fairfax Court House and crossed the Potomac River, already behind schedule.

The brigades moved across Maryland cautiously but unopposed. On June 28 they captured 125 brand new Federal wagons full of forage at Rockville, Maryland. Stuart refused to leave these behind and then spent precious time paroling some 400 prisoners. Pretty girls and captured whiskey further slowed the march. Riding all night, hampered by wagons and more prisoners, Stuart reached Hood's

Mill, Maryland, and then wasted more hours destroying tracks of the Baltimore & Ohio Railroad, and then squandered more time waiting to ambush trains that never came.

Finally, the Confederate raiders moved off to Westminster, Maryland, where they encountered two companies of very stubborn Delaware cavalry, and spent the night spread out on the road from Westminster to Union Mills. Here, Stuart first learned that Federal cavalry under just-promoted Brigadier General Judson Kilpatrick was in pursuit and only seven miles away at Littlestown. Resting his weary troopers, Stuart entered Hanover, Pennsylvania, mid-morning on June 30, where he hotly engaged a brigade of Federal cavalry. After another all-night march the Confederates arrived in Dover, paroled the last of the Federal prisoners and rested on the morning of July 1. They had been constantly on the march for over a week with no communication whatsoever with General Lee and the main army.

The next morning Stuart and his troopers moved on to Dillsburg, still oblivious of the momentous events that were transpiring at Gettysburg. Stuart rode on to Carlisle and shelled and burned the cavalry barracks where he once served. A messenger from Lee's headquarters finally found Stuart at Carlisle about 1:00 AM and urged him toward Gettysburg, still thirty miles away. The courier informed him that the Confederate army was already heavily engaged.

Stuart and his cavalry eventually arrived late in the afternoon of July 2. Allegedly, General Lee made the comment, "Well, General Stuart, you are here at last." General Lee had further harsh words for his errant subordinate but then changed his demeanor. Lee said to Stuart, "Let me ask your help now. We will not discuss this matter longer. Help me fight these people." Lee quickly accepted the damage already done and chose to assume a positive stance, for he knew the services of his loyal cavalry commander would be needed in the future.

Stuart's actions unquestionably had some positive results. His maneuvers distracted two Federal cavalry divisions and required an entire Federal army corps to protect the lines of communications of the Army of the Potomac

to Washington City. Stuart's raiders captured 125 badly needed new wagons full of forage and brought them safely to the army. They rode 250 miles mostly through hostile territory while living off the land, and captured nearly 1,000 prisoners along the route. Stuart's men whipped some of Kilpatrick's Yankee units and immobilized 15,000 men that might have attacked General Ewell's flank, while losing only eighty-nine men, killed, wounded or captured.

Nevertheless, this Confederate raid was not a success and was plagued by multiple failures. Stuart, for whatever reason, disobeyed his initial orders. He allowed his already tardy movements to be unnecessarily slowed by captured material and prisoners. Even with knowledge of Federal pursuit he took no action to speed his march. The most calamitous error was his failure to maintain contact with his commander, and this left the Army of Northern Virginia totally ignorant of Federal troop movements and dispositions in the area. This deprivation of intelligence basically rendered General Lee's army deaf and blind. The result was the disastrous Battle of Gettysburg.

General Lee's first official report of the battle, dated July 30, stated bluntly the specific cause for the loss at Gettysburg was "absence of the cavalry." Stuart's glory-seeking adventure was a major tactical and strategic blunder. He never made this mistake again.

Below: The Confederate cavalry rode miles through gently rolling Maryland and Pennsylvania countryside. This photograph shows piles of forage still in the fields, and the hungry Confederates captured a wagon train of it near Rockville, Maryland. Stuart's unwillingness to leave it behind further slowed his progress.

Quantrill's Massacres

Below left: Captain William T. Anderson, known as "Bloody Bill," had a reputation as one of the most brutal lieutenants who rode with Quantrill. Kansas Union forces were responsible for the deaths of Anderson's father, one sister and the maiming of two other sisters. His antipathy toward his enemies was not ill-founded but his merciless repeated execution of prisoners was unjustified. Refusing to surrender, he was shot down by Union forces in an ambush in northern Missouri in October 1864.

Below right: George Maddox, armed with two Remington New Model Army revolvers and wearing an interestingly decorated hat, said of Southern guerrillas after the war, "…as a general thing the best soldiers we had were boys; they didn't know what fear was." His comments about motivation – "a great many of them were made bad men by the cruel treatment they received at the hands of the Kansas Jayhawkers" – no doubt reflected Anderson's feelings too.

The career and exploits of William Clarke Quantrill and the men who rode with him have been a bottomless well of fascinating historical fact and fiction. Born in Dover, Ohio, in 1839, Quantrill became proficient with firearms and was an excellent marksman at an early age. After finishing school he became a teacher by profession but had the wanderlust and never stayed long in one place. The young man engaged in teaching stints in Illinois, Indiana and Ohio, but there were rumors of theft and murder and he migrated to Kansas in March 1857, never to see his family again. Unsuccessful at farming there, he tried gambling in Kansas and gold prospecting in Colorado, before returning to Kansas. By 1860 he was embroiled in the heated political situation.

Quantrill joined regular Confederate forces in June 1861 and fought with some distinction at the Battle of Lexington, but chafed under army discipline. He organized his own command and successfully attacked a Federal unit in Jackson County, Missouri. By 1862 Quantrill began to attract the rough and ready crowd and some Southern sympathizers to his gang. In March the Federal government recognized Quantrill and his men as terrorists and declared them common outlaws. Therefore, they were no longer considered soldiers entitled to the rights of combatants, and would be shot on sight and hanged if captured.

The group served with regular Confederate units in the capture of Independence, Missouri, on August 11, 1862, and the Confederate government awarded a captain's commission to

Quantrill for his service. Frank James and Jim and Cole Younger joined the band, and Jesse James, still a teenager, joined shortly thereafter. Quantrill visited Richmond, Virginia, over the winter to secure a colonel's commission and, although the legitimacy of his claim to such rank is questionable, he returned to Missouri proudly proclaiming himself "Colonel Quantrill."

Quantrill continued his operations and his command grew with his reputation. These activities were increasingly characterized by personal enmity and bitterness. The incident for which his name will ever be remembered, the sacking of Lawrence, Kansas, and the murder of 150 men and boys occurred on August 21, 1863. The town of 2,000 citizens was not a military objective and had no tactical or strategic importance, but it was a center of abolitionist and pro-Union feeling.

The morning began still, clear and warm. A little after 5:00 AM pistol shots were heard as Quantrill and his lieutenants led some 400 guerrillas hell bent on destruction into the sleeping village. Their purpose was to kill Senator James Lane, a hated abolitionist, and Charles Jennison, leader of the 7th Kansas Jayhawker Cavalry, a unit not unlike Quantrill's bunch but with professed Union sympathies. As they rode into town, Quantrill is alleged to have told his men, "Shoot every soldier you see,

but in no way harm a woman or a child." The guerrillas overran the camp of twenty-two unarmed Federal recruits, and fifty or sixty of the raiders began randomly firing into their tents. As the sleepy men emerged, the mounted guerrillas shot them. The cry was heard, "No quarter for you Federal sons of bitches."

The guerrillas broke up into parties of five to ten men each and proceeded to systematically and deliberately destroy the town. Many guerrillas carried written "death lists" to identify the "Kansas red legs" who were to be shot on sight.

Senator Lane fled into a cornfield in his nightshirt and managed to escape. The guerrillas attacked and robbed civilians in the hotel, after which they burned the building to the ground. Many of the bodies of the dead were also burned. By 9:00 AM the town was in flames visible for thirty miles. The raiders, laden with plunder, rode out due south to begin the long ride back to Missouri. In addition to the loss of life, more than 200 homes and businesses were destroyed – estimated at $2.5 million in damage. The sacking and massacre at Lawrence are considered to be one of the major atrocities that occurred during the Civil War.

Quantrill's band was nearly caught at Baldwin City. Union Brigadier General Thomas Ewing, Jr., brother-in-law of General Sherman,

Above: It is often difficult to separate fact from fiction in the career of the Confederate Missouri guerrilla William Clarke Quantrill, and accounts of the activities of Quantrill and his men remain highly partisan to this day. It is hard to reconcile the bland, open-faced image of the young schoolteacher with stories of wanton murder and atrocities committed by the self-proclaimed colonel in the Confederate uniform.

Below: Quantrill and his band of guerrillas overran the sleeping town of Lawrence, Kansas, early in the morning of August 21, 1863. This dramatized illustration appeared in *Harper's Weekly*. The town had no significance as a military target but was the center of abolitionist activity in the area. This was a raid about retribution for years of "no-holds-barred" bloody guerrilla warfare that simmered between residents of Kansas and Missouri.

Above: There is no doubt that innocent civilians, mostly men and teenage boys, were executed during the raid. The guerrillas controlled the town for most of the day and systematically rounded up citizens they believed to be pro-Union and had abused the Missouri residents. The raid was not a military operation but premeditated murder. Such is the awful nature of guerrilla warfare.

was in pursuit with several hundred cavalrymen well armed with repeating rifles. Quantrill skillfully employed his best-mounted and armed men as his rear guard during the retrograde movement. The chase dragged on all afternoon into the night, with intermittent

contact on the open prairie. The following day Quantrill led his band across the state line into the Missouri woodlands and dispersed, having lost only a handful of men.

Four days later, General Ewing signed General Orders, No. 11, that ordered all 20,000

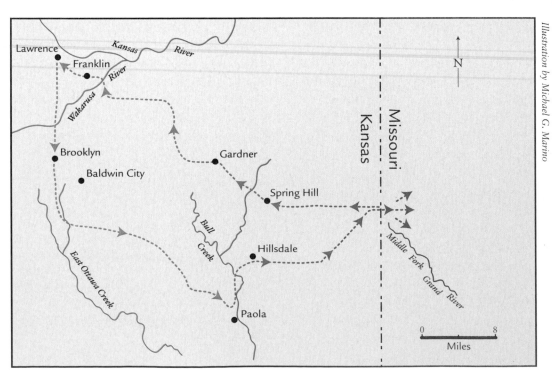

Illustration by Michael G. Marino

Right: Quantrill's legendary loop through Kansas.

Far left: The young men to whom George Maddox referred were not to be mistaken for choirboys. Lieutenant Archie Clements, left seated, Captain David Poole, standing, and William Hendricks had their picture taken in Sherman, Texas, in 1863. The guerrillas pose with cigars and Model 1860 Colt Army revolvers.

Left: Major General James Gillpatrick Blunt was an ardent Kansas Jayhawker before the war and an associate of rabid abolitionist and Lawrence resident Senator James Lane. His despicable reputation was further tarnished by his cowardly desertion of his troops during an encounter with Quantrill near Baxter Springs that resulted in his court martial and relief from command.

people living in Clay, Jackson, Cass and Bates counties, the four border counties, to vacate within fifteen days. All homes were burned and any males apprehended were hanged, introducing a "scorched earth" policy that was total war in every sense of the word. By September 9 the area was desolate. This law was one of the harshest acts of the U.S. government against its own people in American history.

Late in September 1863, Quantrill and his men headed south from Blue Springs toward Indian Territory, where they planned to winter. Riding south on the Ft. Scott road, the band, some 350 strong, captured two Union teamsters who, prior to their execution, told them of a small Union garrison at Baxter Springs. Quantrill devised a plan of attack that used a two-pronged pincer movement. He divided the men with Captain David Poole leading one element and Quantrill commanding the other. Poole's contingent attacked the small post garrisoned by ninety Federal soldiers, most of them black, commanded by Lieutenant James M. Pond. Most of these men stood unarmed in the chow line outside the dirt-and-log fort. The black soldiers broke and

ran, and Poole's men rode them down and shot them at close range. Lieutenant Pond managed to get a mountain howitzer into action and drove the riders off, barely preventing the whole garrison from being slaughtered.

Concurrently, the element with Quantrill approached the little fort from another direction and encountered a Union detachment, about 100 soldiers in a wagon train escorted by Federal cavalry. This was the headquarters of Major General James G. Blunt, relocating the Army of the Frontier from Fort Scott to Fort Smith, Indian Territory. Quantrill's soldiers were outfitted in captured blue Federal uniforms and accouterments. General Blunt initially mistook them to be an honor guard sent out to greet him. He realized his error when raider Captain George Todd led a screaming charge against the formation. Blunt and his mounted escort skedaddled to safety, deserting the wagoners and the band riding in the wagons. These men were summarily executed. Quantrill lost only three men but Union losses were 90 killed and 18 wounded. General Blunt was court-martialed for gross negligence for failing to protect his column, and relieved of

Above: The fabled Western outlaw, Jesse James, honed his skills at age sixteen under the tutelage of Quantrill. The heavily armed teenaged Jesse carried three Colt Army revolvers in this picture. His youth illustrates the observations of George Maddox. Young James joined Quantrill after watching his stepfather being hanged and his mother and sister assaulted by Union troops.

east hoping to join some legitimate Confederate forces.

On January 1, 1865, the marauders crossed back into Missouri and then into Kentucky, where they plundered and burned Kickman and then Danville, where state militia drove them out. Quantrill was surprised at the Wakefield farm near Taylorsville where the group was resting, and he was subsequently wounded and captured. He was taken to a military hospital in Louisville on May 13 and eventually died from wounds on June 6. He was 27 years old.

Quantrill became a member of the Catholic Church as he lay dying in the hospital and left his estate in care of the priest who baptized him. He requested that part of the money be used for a grave plot and the rest be given to Kate King Quantrill, allegedly his wife, although some sources say she was his mistress. Quantrill was buried quietly in St. John's Catholic Cemetery in Louisville in an unmarked grave. One small obituary noted that the "infamous monster" was a captain in the 4th Missouri Cavalry.

Quantrill's remains were buried in Louisville for twenty-two years until 1887. Then an old friend, schoolmate and opportunist from Dover, W. W. Scott, owner and editor of the newspaper, the *Iron Valley Reporter*, with Mrs. Quantrill's acquiescence, convinced the caretaker to open the grave on the pretext of insuring that the remains were actually those of William Clarke Quantrill. The remains were secretly removed to Dover but the town and the local veterans of the Grand Army of the Republic refused to allow burial there. Finally, all parties agreed to the internment in an unmarked grave in 1888. Scott evidently retained the skull and several other bones of Quantrill, and he attempted to sell them several times. Today, the skull is reportedly in the collections of the Dover (Ohio) Historical Society.

Kate opened a boarding house in Louisville, but after four years returned to her family farm in Blue Springs where she died in 1930.

One hundred and ninety-eight men are known to have actually served under Quantrill during the war. Of these, seventy are thought to have been killed in action and only thirty-seven are known to have survived. At least fif-

command upon his arrival at Fort Scott. Quantrill's command continued south into Texas for the winter.

By spring 1864 the band had dwindled to fewer than 100 men and Quantrill temporarily disbanded the group, but they regrouped in September for an ill-advised assault on Fayette, Missouri. The guerrillas were badly beaten and Quantrill began to realize that the war was winding down and his band would be hunted down like common criminals, so they headed

Left: Quantrill guerrilla Captain John Jarrette is armed with three Model 1851 Colt Navy revolvers in this image. Jarrette survived the war but pro-Union vigilantes shot him and his wife in front of their home and then burned their house with their two children inside. The conflict in Missouri and Kansas did not cease just because the Civil War was over. Jarrette's brother-in-law was Cole Younger, another soon-to-be-famous outlaw.

Federal government in 1873 but never brought to trial. A known womanizer, he committed himself to St. Elizabeth's Hospital and Insane Asylum in Washington and died of syphilis on July 21, 1881.

General Ewing, along with his two brothers, ended the war with general's stars, well earned regardless of the family prominence and connections with General Sherman. Ewing declined the posts of Secretary of War and Attorney General under President Johnson, but served two terms in Congress and died in New York in 1896.

Quantrill's guerrillas had their first reunion in 1898 in Independence, Missouri. Later, Frank James and Cole Younger attended annual reunions held every August in Jackson County. President Harry Truman said he attended several later gatherings as a guest and that Quantrill's men were "no more bandits than the men on the other side." It is notable that all the surviving veterans were intensely loyal and unanimously professed admiration and respect for their wartime leader.

The obsession with Quantrill and his associates continues unabated. Several hundred serious books and articles about the subject have already been published and other works are in progress. At least three movies based on aspects of Quantrill's career have appeared on the screen: *Jesse James* starring Henry Fonda in 1939, *Quantrill's Raiders* starring Steve Cochran and Leo Gordon in 1958, and *The Jayhawkers* starring Jeff Chandler in 1959. There is an *Encyclopedia of Quantrill's Guerrillas* and a William Clarke Quantrill Society that has a homepage on the Internet, wcqsociety@aol.com. This is a truly amazing tribute to a man who by most accounts was a pathological killer and has generously been described at best as unprincipled, misguided and misunderstood.

teen of these men went on to become outlaws, the best known being Jesse and Frank James and Cole and Jim Younger. Apparently, others of the group became respected law officers and judges.

Senator James Lane, a target during the raid on Lawrence, found his political career in ruins. Evidently mentally unstable for most of his life, he was confined in an insane asylum near Leavenworth in 1865, where he committed suicide on July 1, 1866.

General Blunt was indicted by the Justice Department for conspiring to defraud the

Below: Survivors of the Lawrence Massacre were photographed by A. Lawrence for the World Wide Company on one of the main streets of Lawrence in 1913, the semi-Centennial Memorial of the event that occurred fifty years before in 1863. Over 200 homes and business were burned in the raids and the flames could be seen for miles.

Early's Scare for President Lincoln

During the summer of 1864, General Grant with Meade's Army of the Potomac was slowly wearing down General Lee's Army of Northern Virginia entrenched around Petersburg. In order to gain some relief, Lee ordered Lieutenant General Jubal Early to take his Second Corps to the Shenandoah Valley, attack the Federal army under Major General David Hunter, and threaten Washington City. Lee hoped this maneuver would force the withdrawal of Union troops from the ever-tightening lines before Petersburg so as to deal with the threat to Washington, and thereby lessen the pressure on Lee's exhausted troops. Early's surreptitious redeployment and subsequent actions came close to changing the outcome of the war.

Early's troops, now called the Army of the Valley District, decisively whipped Hunter's forces near Lynchburg and drove him through the Allegheny Mountains and out of the state. Freed of that Yankee threat, Early left a defensive detachment of 3,000 men and on June 23 led his main force of 14,000 troops on a well planned and executed march down the valley toward Winchester where they arrived July 2, somehow unnoticed by the Federal high command. Early then divided his forces and sent one element against Harpers Ferry and the other toward Martinsburg, West Virginia.

Major General Franz Sigel, commanding the Department of West Virginia, fled Martinsburg on July 3 after only a slight skirmish. The

Right: Major General David Hunter was threatening Lynchburg after his destruction of Lexington, Virginia. Early's troops assaulted Hunter with such force that not only was his command driven from the Lynchburg area but out of the state into the mountains of West Virginia. Major General John B. Gordon and his Georgia Brigade played an important role in smashing Hunter.

Below left: Lieutenant General Jubal A. Early was an eccentric and profane confirmed bachelor that General Lee often called "my bad old man." Nevertheless, Lee found him to be one of his best officers in the field. Lee entrusted "Old Jube" with the task of ridding the valley of troops under General David Hunter and inflicting whatever damage he could. In the end Early nearly captured Washington City and President Lincoln.

Far right: Major General John B. Gordon and his brigade were detached from the Richmond defenses and sent to reinforce Jubal Early's army in the valley. Elements of Gordon's brigade were instrumental in crushing Hunter and later performed admirably at the Monocacy, helping to dislodge Federal units under Lew Wallace.

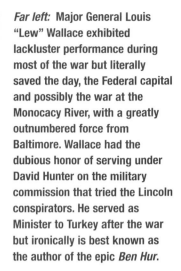

Far left: Major General Louis "Lew" Wallace exhibited lackluster performance during most of the war but literally saved the day, the Federal capital and possibly the war at the Monocacy River, with a greatly outnumbered force from Baltimore. Wallace had the dubious honor of serving under David Hunter on the military commission that tried the Lincoln conspirators. He served as Minister to Turkey after the war but ironically is best known as the author of the epic *Ben Hur*.

Above left: In this sketch by A. R. Waud the destroyed railroad bridge and the wooden bridge on the Georgetown Road across the Monacacy River mark the key terrain feature along which General Lew Wallace deployed his outnumbered Federal troops to contest the onslaught of Early's Confederates. Wallace's stubborn and heroic resistance slowed the Confederate advance for twenty-four crucial hours, allowing General Grant time to withdraw troops at Petersburg and rush them north to the nearly empty defenses around the Federal capital.

and the infantry divisions of Wharton, Gordon, Ramseur and Rodes. General Wallace selected a strong defensive position for his numerically inferior force some thirty miles northwest of the capital. Reinforcements – Major General James B. Ricketts' Third Division, part of General Wright's VI Corps – arrived in the nick of time to block a flanking maneuver by General John McCausland's Confederate cavalry, and increased the number of Union troops to over 6,000. These men stopped five determined Confederate assaults on July 9, temporarily impeding the Confederate advance on an almost undefended Washington. Union losses were 1,880 men killed, wounded or captured.

Wallace's troops burned a strategic wooden highway bridge and conducted an orderly

Yankees also evacuated Harpers Ferry during the night of July 4 after burning the bridges. Excited and confident Confederate forces crossed the Potomac River on July 6. New orders from Lee to Early detached the cavalry brigade of Colonel Bradley T. Johnson to threaten Baltimore, cut communications, and attempt the liberation of 18,000 Confederate prisoners of war then at Point Lookout, Maryland.

Early encouraged the city fathers of Hagerstown, Maryland, to pay $20,000 or see the town reduced to ashes. The good citizens of Frederick, presented with similar options, coughed up $200,000. General Early then marched southeast to the Monocacy River where he unexpectedly found Northern troops entrenched and ready to fight. By that point, Early's men had marched over 300 miles in less than twenty-five days and were tired and behind schedule.

The Yankees in Early's way were veteran Federal troops under Major General Lewis "Lew" Wallace, commanding the Middle Department based in Baltimore, who had advanced to meet the Confederate threat. Early's larger force consisted of Imboden's and McCausland's cavalry

Left: Brigadier General John Daniel Imboden, shown here in civilian clothes, led raids that almost brought the Baltimore & Ohio Railroad to a standstill. He commanded a brigade of cavalry during Early's operations against Washington City and his units helped find a ford across the Monocacy that enabled Southern forces to assault the Federal flank and force Wallace's withdrawal toward Baltimore.

Right: This house behind the Federal lines on the Seventh Street road near Fort Stevens shows the effect of shelling by Early's artillery during the Confederate attempt to enter Washington from the northwest. President Lincoln and his family had moved to the grounds of the Soldier's Home nearby to escape the summer heat in the city.

withdrawal toward Baltimore that evening, having delayed Early's men for a whole crucial day. Early realized at this point that the Federal high command fully appreciated the danger his army posed and was reacting to face the threat.

Early finally reached Silver Springs on July 11, slowed by nine miles of supply train, a number of wounded and 300 prisoners. He marched his staggering, strung-out regiments down the Seventh Street turnpike to the Washington defenses at Fort Stevens that afternoon, but found his army too hot and tired to mount a concerted assault. The men commented on the intense heat and suffocating clouds of dust on the approach march. It caused so many stragglers that only about 8,000 men were present when they reached the fort. General Early and advance elements of the 62nd Virginia Mounted Infantry approached the defenses around mid-day and saw that the works were defended only by a skeleton force. Here was the opportunity of a lifetime.

Meanwhile, official Washington was hysterical. Grossly inflated estimates of Confederate

troop strength ranged from 30,000 to 50,000 men, and the Federal government was contemplating moving all records to New York. Reports indicated that Wallace's army had been totally annihilated and the remaining male population of the city went on a major booze-up.

Major General Christopher C. Auger, in command of the Department of Washington, had fewer than 5,000 men to man thirty-seven miles of defensive positions that encircled the capital, and many of these were disabled men of the Veteran Reserve Corps, clerks and quartermaster types, and even some 100-day, untrained, emergency troops. Some of the fortifications mounted large siege and garrison pieces of artillery that this motley crew had no idea how to serve. Subsequent fire from these batteries would prove harmless and inaccurate at best.

Literally while Early's advance party watched, Wright's veteran Federal troops, the remainder of the VI Corps, arrived and filed into the empty defenses. President and Mrs. Lincoln, visiting their nearby summer residence, were at the fort and witnessed Wright's arrival and Early's first assaults.

Right: Federal fear of Confederate incursions into Washington City prompted General Herman Haupt to have his Construction Corps fortify all rail yards and shops around the city. This fortification at the Orange and Alexandria Railroad yards is typical of the defenses that surrounded the city and confronted General Jubal Early's Confederates in the summer of 1864.

Right: Fort Slemmer, with its earthen parapet, brush abatis and barbette-mounted 32-pounder guns, was the type of Federal fortification that Early's hot and thirsty men approached northwest of Washington, near Silver Springs, Maryland. Luckily for the Confederates, the gun crews were untrained and incompetent and did little damage

By mid-afternoon the situation had drastically changed. Confederate forces actively probed the Yankee defenses until sunset and lost about 700 men killed and wounded. After dark, Early and his command staff met at a local mansion, the Blair House, to plan further offensive action. Regrettably for the Confederate effort, the night was wasted when the officers attacked a cellar full of rum rather than the still shaky Federal positions.

The next morning all the heavy siege guns were manned and the lines were full of Union troops. Nevertheless, the Confederates remained in position and maintained a constant fire on Federal defenses. President Lincoln returned to the fort later in the afternoon and walked up on the parapet accompanied by General Wright until driven to cover by accurate small arms fire. Both sides kept up heavy skirmishing and probing after dark until 10:00 PM, when Early decided he had done all he could do.

The Confederates began a withdrawal during the night and General Wright was criticized for his timid pursuit rather than praised for his timely arrival. General Grant was loudly denounced for having allowed Early to get loose in the valley and then refusing to come north himself. The Confederates easily reached safety with all their captured booty and eventually rejoined Lee.

General Early said, "We haven't taken Washington, but we've scared Abe Lincoln like hell." And he was right. General Wallace later said, "These men died to save the National Capital, and they did save it." There is little doubt that had Early not been detained by Wallace's heroic holding action at Monocacy, he could have waltzed into Washington. One question argued over since is what impact would the capture of President Lincoln and the cabinet have had on the outcome of the war?

The affair at Fort Stevens is the only occasion of an American president being involved in a battle while in office. The president could very easily have been killed or captured. It was a real close thing.

Above left: **The Long Bridge ran across the Potomac River to Alexandria and was the primary connection to northern Virginia. Eventually, the U.S. Military Railroad would construct a railroad span beside it. The approach at both ends of the bridge was heavily guarded to prevent Confederate raiders from charging into the city. Jubal Early did just that, but approached from the northeast.**

Above: **When Early pulled his exhausted troops back from Washington into the Shenandoah Valley he faced fresh Union forces under General Phil Sheridan. "Little Phil" followed "Old Jube's" withdrawing Confederates relentlessly and, during September and October, fought the battles of Third Winchester, Fisher's Hill and Cedar Creek, effectively smashing Confederate forces in the valley.**

Left: **During the Confederate withdrawal back into Virginia, General Early ordered Brigadier General John McCausland to take his brigade of cavalry to Chambersburg, Pennsylvania, and demand restitution of $500,000 for depredations in the valley committed by David Hunter, whom they had just thoroughly thrashed. Failing to meet Confederate demands, the city was burned. Chambersburg received compensation for this episode from the Federal government as late as the 1970s.**

Forrest's Raid on Memphis

Below left: Major General Nathan Bedford Forrest has been described as an untutored military genius and the finest cavalry officer of both sides during the Civil War. He was already a local legend by the second year of the war. General Lee was once asked who he thought was the greatest soldier of the war. His reply was, "A man I have never seen, sir. His name is Forrest."

Below center: Major General Andrew Jackson Smith may have become over-confident after besting Forrest's men at Tupelo in July. When Smith's column rode out of Memphis they had every intention of confronting Forrest in a conventional engagement, but were unable to find the elusive Confederates who had already slipped behind them, moving toward Memphis.

Far right: Major General Cadwallader Colden Washburn was incredibly more successful as an entrepreneur and politician than as a military commander. He amassed a fortune before the war and afterward was a founder of the company that became General Mills. His political connections, President Lincoln and General Grant, served him well during a mediocre but competent period in service.

Nathan Bedford Forrest was already a legend in both armies by 1864, and the mere mention of his name was cause for great concern among his Federal adversaries.

In August 1864, Union Major General A. J. Smith, already well acquainted with Forrest since the Battle of Tupelo, led 16,000 Federal infantry and 3,000 cavalry with artillery support southeast out of Memphis to confront Forrest's cavalry south of the Tallahatchie River. But he just couldn't get the elusive Confederates to fight a pitched battle. The gray-clad soldiers always disappeared like smoke. Forrest knew he could not fight the numerically superior Northerners on even terms so he concentrated his units near Oxford on August

18 and planned a raid around the right (western) flank of General Smith's forces. The objective was Memphis, with a garrison of about 6,000 troops and Major General Cadwallader C. Washburn, Commander of the Department of West Tennessee, and his subordinate, Major General Stephen A. Hurlburt, commander of the XVI Army Corps, and Brigadier General Ralph P. Buckland, Commander of the District of Memphis, all of whom were headquartered there. Forrest left Chalmers' Brigade to demonstrate in front of General Smith and keep his attention.

On Monday, August 22, 1864, some sixty miles behind the oblivious Smith and his Yankee troops, General Forrest with 1,500 troopers, elements of Bell's and Neely's Brigades and

Morton's Battery, rode up the Hernando Road through Nonconnah Bottoms in fog and pouring rain. Captain William Forrest, the general's brother, led the advance party in a column of fours about a mile ahead of the main body. It was pitch black dark. Lead elements of the Confederates, riding at a fast canter, found the first Yankee vidette on top of a hill near the old Poston House. When challenged, the advance party announced they were elements of the 7th Illinois Cavalry returning from a scout. One member of the party went forward to deal with the guard, but his revolver misfired because of the weather and the troopers behind him shot the guard and overran the picket post before the Union soldiers could get out of their blankets. Soon after, the Confederates passed a large group of 90-day militia in a camp near the Ford house, but these Union soldiers didn't believe they were really Forrest's Confederate cavalry and let them pass unopposed.

The riders approached the Provine place near the Stewart house and found a Federal battery that immediately surrendered after several pistol shots were fired. The Yankee artillerymen were quick to tell the raiders that a regiment of black troops were in barracks in the hollow just ahead. The Confederate troopers told the artillerymen not to go away and then galloped through the barracks shooting wildly in the dark.

Lieutenant Colonel Jesse Forrest and his force went after General Washburn. The general fled in his nightshirt to Fort Pickering on the bluff, leaving his wife alone in bed to face the Southern gentlemen. Confederate troopers

seeking General Buckland narrowly missed the general as he ran out the back door of his residence. Captain Forrest and his group went on to Gayoso House hotel to capture General Hurlburt. The party literally rode their horses into the lobby of the hotel and captured the

Above: This particular saddle is known as the Morgan Muley pattern and utilizes oversize bent wood stirrups. This pattern was commonly found in the northern Mississippi and west Tennessee area in years past. This type of saddle seems to have been preferred rather than other makes in some western army mounted units.

Left: Harper's Weekly gave ample coverage to Forrest's audacious raid into Memphis, Federal headquarters for the Department of West Tennessee, the District of Memphis and the XVI Army Corps, garrisoned by some 6,000 troops. Elements of Forrest's raiding party attempted to nab General Hurlburt in his bed at Gayoso House but were unsuccessful.

desk clerk and a Union officer. They dismounted, broke into a cigar stand and lit up cigars. The Union officer exclaimed in a pompous manner that, when he surrendered he thought the men were soldiers, "but now I see that you are a lot of damned guerrillas." One of the Confederate raiders drew his revolver and threatened to shoot the obnoxious officer, but Captain Forrest stopped him and told the Union officer he should leave the hotel and mind his manners. Shortly thereafter, someone shot him anyway. A search of the entire hotel failed to turn up the Yankee general.

Some twenty troopers from Captain Forrest's group went over to the Federal Irving Block prison to release the captives, but the place was well defended. They pounded on the door with carbine butts but could not enter. Federal small arms fire from the second story windows, and pockets of Union resistance on Second Street, forced the Confederates to withdraw.

Union gunboats at the base of the levee stood out to mid-river to make sure the rampaging Confederates did not board them. Forrest's men occupied the telegraph office and had a fine time sending disinformation up and down the line. They announced that Forrest and 10,000 men had captured the town. St. Louis and Cincinnati garrisons were put on alert and Chicago called up 20,000 local militia. The civilian population went wild with excitement because the boys in gray were back, if only for a short time.

General Forrest and the main force with Morton's Battery had stopped to engage the Federals encamped around the State Female College on McLemore Street. A hard fight ensued until the Confederates realized there were still women in residence. By 9:00 AM General Forrest knew he had failed to capture the three generals and Federal resistance was beginning to organize. The bugle sounded recall and Forrest headed back south with Captain Forrest and his group as rear guard.

The Confederates had occupied the town for four hours. Forrest captured over 600 prisoners and 80 horses. The Federals lost 15 killed and 65 wounded. While the Southerners had not captured any Federal generals, they seized General Washburn's uniform and sword. General Smith, floundering around north Mississippi, received a plaintive dispatch from General Washburn:

"We were attacked at 3 0'clock this morning by a force of cavalry said to have been led by Forrest in person…You will at once order all your cavalry to move to intercept them…They must be cut off and caught. Move rapidly and spare not horse flesh."

Smith and his command chased all over northern Mississippi and back to the defenses of Memphis with no success. The elusive Forrest had disappeared again.

After the Confederates were safely away, later that afternoon under a flag of truce, Forrest sent back seriously ill Federal soldiers and also returned Washburn's uniform and sword. Washburn gallantly responded by sending some fine gray cloth, buttons and gold lace for uniforms for Forrest and his staff.

As the dust settled General Hurlburt supposedly said, "Well, they have removed me from command because I couldn't keep Forrest out of West Tennessee; but apparently Washburn can't keep him out of his bedroom."

An exceptional bronze equestrian statue of General Forrest, unveiled in 1905, marks the gravesite of the general and Mrs. Forrest in Forrest Park in downtown Memphis. Repeated attempts by various groups to have the remains of the general and his wife and the statue removed have been notably unsuccessful.

Above left: Major General Stephen Augustus Hurlburt was more interested in lining his pockets rather than fighting anyone, including General Forrest by the time he came to Memphis. His blatant black market and illegal cotton dealings were outrageous and he was almost arrested but eventually was "mustered out with honor." Charges of drunkenness and corruption followed him for the rest of his life.

Above: Confederate forces attempted to free prisoners held in the Irving Block Prison but were repulsed by stubborn Union defenders reinforced by elements of the 8th Iowa quartered nearby. Forrest soon realized that stiffening Federal resistance was becoming more organized and prudently ordered his forces to begin an orderly withdrawal.

Above: This Confederate-manufactured cavalry saber has a sheet-iron-mounted wooden scabbard in order to economize on scarce metal and facilitate manufacture by unskilled labor. This example was made around Atlanta and would have been available to Forrest's cavalry. Surviving ordnance returns of Forrest's units indicate they preferred longarms and revolvers.

Hampton's Beefsteak Raid

Below: Hampton managed the dwindling Confederate cavalry resources well. Personally fearless, he believed in leading from the front and was wounded three times during the war. Hampton suggested the raid on the Union beef herd to General Lee who readily approved the unusual military operation. Hampton was promoted to the rank of lieutenant general before the end of the war.

Major General Wade Hampton commanded Confederate cavalry of the Army of Northern Virginia after the death of Major General J.E.B. Stuart, who was mortally wounded at Yellow Tavern during Sheridan's raid on Richmond. Late summer 1864 found Confederate cavalry indulging in a brief but much needed period of rest and recuperation. Federal cavalry under Brigadier Generals David M. Gregg and Au-gust V. Kautz had cautiously advanced closer to Petersburg, leaving the Union rear and Grant's headquarters at City Point dangerously exposed. Besides the deteriorating military situation, General Lee was well aware that his army was already on short rations and faced a winter that would bring near starvation.

Sergeant George Shadburne, attached to the Jeff Davis Legion, was one of the most aggressive scouts in the army and reported directly to General Hampton. He made an extremely fortuitous discovery on one his frequent ventures behind Federal lines. On September 5 he returned from a clandestine foray with the intelligence that a large herd, "3,000 beeves, attended by 120 men and 30 citizens, without arms," were corralled near Coggin's Point on the James River, south of Richmond, less than twenty-five miles from Hampton's headquarters. Shadburne advised that Federal cavalry pickets were along the river, but at least two miles from the herd. The cattle were ripe for the taking and Hampton proposed to take them. General Lee quickly saw an easy way to solve his immediate food supply needs and embarrass Federal authorities, and approved the plan.

Hampton devised a three-pronged operation. Rooney Lee and elements of his division would demonstrate to the west of Sycamore Church, while Dearing's Brigade did the same to the east. Hampton, led by his trusty scout, Shadburne, with Rosser's brigade, would deal with Federal pickets at Sycamore Church and then go for beef. The remaining elements of Dunovant and Young left behind would keep up a constant show of force to distract the Federals.

After a week of careful planning, on the morning of September 14, Hampton led 4,000 men from bivouacs along the Weldon Railroad around the left flank of General Meade's Army

of the Potomac. The force consisted of the Barringer and Chambliss brigades of Major General W. H. F. "Rooney" Lee's division, Brigadier General Thomas L. Rosser's famed Laurel Brigade, Brigadier General James Dearing's brigade, and a detachment of 100 men from the brigades of P. B. M. Young and John Dunovant, all of Major General M. C. Butler's division, and a detail of forty hand-picked men under two officers, armed with pistols and axes, serving as a "mounted engineer troop."

The bugle sounded "boots and saddles" way before dawn. Initially, the long column moved down the Boydton Plank Road to Dinwiddie Court House, then turned southeast, across the Weldon Railroad to Wilkinson's Bridge on Rowanty creek, where they camped for the night. The raiders resumed the march at dawn, traveling northeast to the Jerusalem Plank Road and then on back roads to the Blackwater River. They covered thirty-eight miles, undetected, in two days, and the scratch pioneer unit reconstructed the destroyed Cooke's Bridge, thus allowing the riders to cross the river that night. They stopped to rest and prepare for action at 3:30 AM in the rear of the Federal army.

At 5:00 AM, yelling and shooting troopers of Rosser's Laurel Brigade overran elements of the 1st District of Columbia Cavalry at Sycamore Church. In less than thirty minutes they killed, captured or wounded 219 of the 250 men present, seizing their coveted Henry Rifles and fine horses. Hampton, with Rosser, covered the four miles to Coggin's Point by 6:00 AM, encountering little resistance. The civilian drovers tried to scatter the herd but the Confederates captured the cattle and attendant commissary and sutlers' stores. Troopers of Rooney Lee and Dearing held the roads on either flank and cut the telegraph. Lee's Division

Above: The amount of forage needed to feed all the horses, mules and beef used by the Federal army was staggering. This government storage area in Alexandria shipped forage by water to City Point to the huge depot there. The impoverished Confederates were well aware of this immense, ever-growing horde of supplies so close to their lines.

Left: The massive Federal supply depot at City Point, Virginia, with its docks, storage facilities and rail spurs, supplied General Grant's Federal army in the summer and fall of 1864 as the Union forces hammered at the defenses of Richmond and Petersburg. All the hardtack, canned food and herds of beef that fed the Union army were here, a tempting target for the ill-fed and poorly equipped Confederates.

Right: Brigadier General Matthew Calbraith Butler had been colonel of the 2nd South Carolina Cavalry and lost a foot at Brandy Station. Butler was Hampton's brother-in-law and served under him throughout the war. Like some other former Confederates, he put back on the blue uniform and served as general officer in the Spanish-American War in 1898.

swooped down on the sleeping camps of the 3rd New York Cavalry and elements of the 11th Pennsylvania Cavalry and the remainder of the 1st District of Columbia Cavalry. Most of the groggy Union troopers surrendered in their nightclothes, but some managed to escape into the woods.

By 8:00 AM Hampton, still with Rosser and his troopers, had the herd under control and headed for Confederate lines. Union gunboats on the James River joined in, throwing shells after the whooping Confederate cowboys. With 2,000 Federal cavalry, Brigadier General Henry Davies, Jr., began the pursuit of the withdrawing raiders on Jerusalem Plank Road, but the Confederates had an overwhelming head start and actually outnumbered the Federal pursuers.

Yankees under Davies and the Confederates under Rosser collided around 4:00 PM near Ebenezer Church. Dearing's and Lee's formations reinforced Rosser, and a running fight ensued that lasted about four hours. At dark both antagonists disengaged and retired.

Confusion had been the order of the day at various Federal headquarters. Initial reports said that Confederate cavalry had broken the Union line and were headed for the huge supply depot at City Point. The usual inflated strength estimates announced Hampton had 14,000 cavalry. Another report said Confederates had ten regiments of infantry and at least a battery of eight guns. It was noon before some semblance of organization appeared. General Kautz and his 700-man contingent

managed to round up eighteen steers that had strayed from the stolen herd.

The rustled cattle herd, on another road south of the main party, stretched for seven miles under an immense cloud of dust. They crossed over the Blackwater River bridge and then the Nottoway River at Freeman's Ford and Rowanty Creek on Wilkinson's Bridge, reaching Petersburg unmolested at around 9:00 AM on the morning of August 17.

The Southern cavalry had ridden almost 100 miles during this unusual operation. They captured 304 very well armed Federal soldiers including some telegraphers, plus three guidons, ordnance stores, small arms and wagons. Confederate losses were 10 killed, 47 wounded and 10 missing. Rosser proudly boasted that they "delivered to Gen-eral Lee's commissary every one of the 2,486 beeves."

This escapade was the only officially sanctioned incident of cattle rustling during the Civil War, and evidently was grudgingly appreciated even by those who wore the blue. General Grant was subsequently asked when he expected to starve out Lee, and the Northern general replied, "Never, if our armies continue to supply him with beef-cattle." President Lincoln wryly remarked that the raid was "the slickest piece of cattle stealing."

No monuments or memorials commemorate this particular footnote in history, but Hollywood produced a movie in 1966, *Alvarez Kelly,* starring William Holden and Richard Widmark, loosely based on Hampton's great beefsteak raid.

Above: **Artist A. R. Waud's illustration depicts Hampton's Confederate troopers driving approximately 2,500 head of cattle, the whole Union beef herd rustled at Coggin's Point, back to Confederate lines. After the episode Confederate pickets jokingly thanked the Federal pickets for sharing their meat rations. The Federals responded by thanking them for taking the tough old beef that had followed the army all summer.**

Left: **Major General Wade Hampton led what was left of Confederate Cavalry Corps after General Stuart's death. A personally wealthy individual before the war, he outfitted the Hampton Legion at his own expense with short Enfield rifles and artillery imported from England. This jeweler-made, gold, two-piece South Carolina state seal belt plate was part of this aristocratic soldier's accouterments.**

The St. Albans Bank Robberies

Below: At the St. Albans Bank, after a verbal confrontation, one of the raiders, Collins, ordered the captives to raise their right hands and "solemnly swear to obey and respect the Constitution of the Confederate States of America." One of the witnesses later said the raiders smelled strongly of alcohol.

On several occasions during the war the Confederate government gave serious consideration to operations against Northern states from Canada. In April 1864 President Jefferson Davis appointed Clement C. Clay, J. P. Holcombe and Jacob Thompson as Confederate Commissioners to Canada, and authorized the men to encourage an insurrection among Southern sympathizers, Copperheads, in Indiana, Illinois and Ohio, and to formulate plans for the liberation of Confederate prisoners of war held at Camp Douglas near Chicago and Johnson's Island near Sandusky, Ohio. Word of these plans leaked to Federal authorities and resulted in increased vigilance along the border.

Clay and Thompson enlisted the aid of Captain Thomas Hines, one of Morgan's raiders, who had escaped from the Federal prison in Ohio, to lead the Camp Douglas operation scheduled for late August. The plan was discovered due to poor security, and Federal authorities arrested most of those involved.

Clay was also deeply involved with Lieutenant Bennett H. Young, another of Morgan's ill-fated Ohio raiders who had escaped, and assisted Young in the planning and funding of the raid on banks in St. Albans, Vermont, in October 1864. Lieutenant Young met with Clay at St. Catherines, Canada, in September and received initial funding of $400 shortly thereafter. Young and members of his force made several

reconnaissances to St. Albans and carefully noted the locations of the banks, livery stables, gun stores and other strategic points. Young was even given a tour of Governor John Gregory Smith's residence in the town. Clay eventually provided a total of $2,462 in funding for the raiders for this particular operation.

Young's assault party of some twenty-five men inconspicuously infiltrated the town, just fifteen miles south of the Canadian border, on Lake Champlain. They arrived by train in small groups, beginning on October 10. Most of the men were young Kentuckians, innocuously dressed and each carrying one shoulder bag or valise concealing their arms and equipment. The men were friendly and mingled easily with the townspeople who thought they were visiting hunters. The whole party was soon in place, quartered at three hotels, Tremont House, American House and St. Albans House. Continued reconnaissance alerted the party to the fact that every Tuesday was

market day, so the operation was planned for Wednesday, when the town would be quieter.

On October 19, when the town clock struck 3:00 PM, three assault teams simultaneously entered the St. Albans Bank, the Franklin County Bank and the 1st National Bank of St. Albans, and proclaimed that they were Confederate soldiers acting in retribution for Union atrocities committed by Generals Sherman and Sheridan within the Confederacy. All the men were dressed in civilian attire, with no Confederate uniforms in evidence.

The raiders found the limited amounts of gold and silver too heavy to carry but seized a total of $208,000 in various forms of currency from the three banks. Meanwhile, a fourth group herded the incredulous populace at gunpoint onto the village green, and confiscated all available horses. The telegrapher at St. Albans managed to send a message that reached Governor Smith in the capital at Montpelier that read, "Southern raiders are in town, robbing

Above: The raid on St. Albans received ample graphic coverage in the November 14, 1864, issue of *Frank Leslie's Illustrated Newspaper.* One of its artists produced a sequence of illustrations depicting the raid based on eyewitness accounts. This view shows how designated assault teams entered each bank and identified themselves as Confederate soldiers, stating that their raid was in retribution for Federal actions in the Shenandoah Valley. Bank personnel were threatened with immediate death if they did not promptly turn over all funds to the raiders.

banks, shooting citizens and burning houses." Then, the line went dead.

By 3:30 PM Lieutenant Young had accomplished his primary mission and ordered his men to fire the town. The group carried numerous four-ounce bottles of an incendiary chemical mixture called "Greek Fire" that they threw against buildings, but the concoction malfunctioned and no fire started.

Some isolated residents resisted. Elias J. Morrison was mortally wounded during the scattered shooting and died three days later. Collins H. Huntington and another civilian were wounded during the round-up of the townspeople. Captain George P. Conger, a recently returned veteran, evaded capture by running out of the back of American House and raised the alarm.

Lieutenant Young realized that resistance was being organized and ordered his party to mount up. He led his men at the gallop north on the Sheldon Road to the Canadian border and safety. Plans to seize the Sheldon Bank on the way were frustrated because the bank was closed as they clattered past. The Confederates managed to fire two bridges, but Conger and his hastily gathered posse of townspeople were so close behind that they extinguished the flames and kept after the fleeing party to Frelighsburg, Quebec, where the raiders just disappeared. Another posse led by a Captain Newton also failed to cut off the escaping raiders.

The Confederate party assumed they were safe in Canada, but Alamanda P. Bruce, Thomas B. Collins, James A. Doty, Samuel S. Gregg, Joseph McGrorty, William H. Hutchinson, Samuel E. Lackey, Dudley Moore, George Scott, Marcus Spurr, Charles M. Swager, Squire T. Teavis, Caleb M. Wallace and Young were subsequently arrested by Canadian authorities at several locations.

On October 21, the U.S. Secretary of State, William H. Seward, demanded the immediate extradition of the bank robbers under the provisions of the Webster-Ashburton Treaty. The Governor General of Canada, Lord Charles Stanley Monck, countered and ordered the men jailed in Montreal, where they were brought to trial on November 7. Commissioner Clay hired three prominent Canadian attorneys for the sum of $6,000 and, after due diligence and considerable politicking, the Canadian court received documentation from the Confederate government in Richmond that the raiders were in fact Southern soldiers acting under orders. On December 13, the prisoners were discharged because the arrest warrant had been deemed defective, to the howls of frustration from Federal authorities. The fact that all those in custody were Confederate soldiers who had been captured by Union forces and subsequently escaped played some part in the Canadian determination of their legal status. Some

of the men were re-arrested several times, only to have charges dismissed before they finally sailed for Europe. By then Clay had spent some $500,000 in Canada that had no impact on the outcome of the war.

Legal wrangling continued until April 1865, when the Canadian government returned some of the seized bank notes and made other restitution in gold to the three banks. The U.S. Congress passed an act abrogating the legal reciprocity treaty with Canada, and threatened to abrogate the treaty between the two countries detailing disarmament on the Great Lakes, but cooler heads prevailed and the situation calmed with the passage of time, although both governments stationed additional troops along the joint border for quite a while.

Hollywood recognized the drama of the incident and in 1954 produced *The Raid*, star-

ring Van Heflin, Richard Boone and Lee Marvin. In this case the plot actually had some strong basis in historical fact. Today, the quiet little town of 7,650 inhabitants is the home of the annual Maple Festival and proclaims itself to be the site of the northern-most engagement of the Civil War.

Above: This photograph of the raiders taken in the Montreal Jail definitely shows the men in some sort of uniform. Most wear shell jackets with brass buttons and high boots. Left to right, standing, are Reverend Stephen Cameron, George Scott and Squire Turner Teavis; and seated are William Huntley Hutchinson, George N. Sanders and the leader, Lieutenant Bennett H. Young.

Left: This photograph, one of a sequence taken on December 27, 1864, in front of the Montreal Jail by pioneer Canadian photographer William Notman, shows some of the raiders who were re-arrested after their initial dismissal. Lieutenant Bennett H. Young, leader of the group, stands to the far right wearing a gray coat.

Rosser's Winter Successes

Below left: Major General Thomas L. Rosser commanded the 5th Virginia Cavalry until his promotion in the fall of 1863. Subsequently, in command of the Laurel Brigade, he earned a reputation as one of the leading Confederate cavalry officers of the war. Promoted major general on November 4, 1864, he refused to surrender at Appomattox and, with two regiments, broke through Union lines. Rosser was another Confederate who put on the blue uniform again and was a brigadier general of U.S. Volunteers in the Spanish-American War in 1898.

Below right: Union Colonel George R. Latham, 5th West Virginia Cavalry, was the unfortunate commander of the Union garrison at the vast supply depot at New Creek, West Virginia. The installation, located on a ridge at the end of a narrow valley between two mountains, was considered one of the most secure in the area. Colonel Latham was forewarned of the presence of Rosser's raiders in the area but inexplicably chose to take no defensive precautions.

November 28, 1864: New Creek, West Virginia

One of the primary Union supply lines was the Baltimore & Ohio Railroad. The line was attacked repeatedly in efforts to disrupt the flow of supplies to the fighting men of the Federal army. Eventually, a line of fortified blockhouses, repair stations and supply depots dotted the railroad, garrisoned by thousands of troops, to protect it from the incessantly marauding Confederate raiders and guerrillas.

The installation that sprang up around New Creek, West Virginia, was considered one of the best fortified and most secure of these military cantonments. The actual fortification was located at the intersection of the New Creek and Potomac River Valleys and occupied a narrow ridge between two prominent elevations. Fort Kelley boasted a garrison of around 800 men and five pieces of field artillery. There was only one approach corridor, the narrow New Creek Valley, and previous Confederate efforts to assault the place had failed. New Creek was considered impregnable, and the garrison became overconfident and complacent.

On November 26, 1864, Confederate Major General Thomas L. Rosser left camps in the Shenandoah Valley with his old command, the Laurel Brigade, and another brigade of cavalry, about 600 men, and rode north on an operation against the unwary garrison in West Virginia. Around Moorefield, the next day, the Confederates stumbled into a 300-man Federal detachment from New Creek. A running skirmish ensued and most of the frightened Federals escaped and headed back to alert the garrison. Rosser feared he had lost all secrecy and surprise, but ordered his men to ride all night in the hope of arriving ahead of the escaping Federals.

The gray raiders halted at dawn just six miles from the objective and, after a brief council of war, all agreed to proceed with the assault. The mounted Confederates advanced slowly, led by Major Thomas Sweeney and a small advanced guard wearing Federal overcoats. The group rode right up to the forward Federal pickets and easily captured them without firing a shot. Riding on, they captured a second picket post only two miles from the fort, with similar ease. To their amazement, the raiders were able to easily penetrate to the base of the ridge on which the installation sat without being engaged. By then it was daylight, and Rosser expected to be discovered at any minute.

Rosser and his men split into three assault groups. One element went for the infantry camp to the left, while a second went straight for the railroad depot and telegraph lines, and the third made for the artillery battery on the right. They charged, expecting to encounter stiff resistance, only to find a skeleton crew of sentries walking post. The remaining members of the garrison were on mess call or relaxing in the camp area. The post commander, Colonel George R. Latham, 5th West Virginia Cavalry,

for some inexplicable reason had failed to alert his garrison of the presence of Confederate cavalry headed his way. In less than half an hour Rosser and his raiders bagged the fort, the stupefied colonel, and more than 700 dazed soldiers.

In addition to the prisoners, the Confederates seized 500 cattle and 200 horses, and plundered tons of supplies and burned the storage buildings. Then, Rosser, for another inexplicable reason, left the railroad and strategic bridge undamaged and rode off into the woods late in the afternoon. The Confederate cavalry was safely back in camp by December 6 with supplies sufficient for several weeks.

In January 1865 Colonel Latham was court-martialed, found guilty of neglect of duty, and dishonorably discharged. Two months later, Latham, by then a politician, a Republican Congressman, had his dismissal revoked and wangled a retroactive honorable discharge from the service.

January 6-11, 1865: Beverly, West Virginia

By January 1865, the Shenandoah Valley lay in ruins. Federal General Sheridan had destroyed everything, and food shortages were so critical that some Confederate units were temporarily disbanded and sent home for lack of food for men and forage for animals. Major General Rosser's cavalry brigade was one formation still active, albeit half-clothed, armed with captured weapons and poorly mounted. Rosser, huddled in camps around Staunton, Virginia, received intelligence that just seventy-five miles north of him in Beverly, West Virginia, was a Federal supply depot bulging with food and supplies, and guarded by only 1,000 Yankees.

Rosser requested and received permission to mount a raid on the place. The weather was horrible, with numbing cold and deep snow all over the area. Rosser asked for volunteers from his destitute command to undertake this hazardous mission and some 300 brave souls answered the call. These volunteers were divided into two elements of 150 men each, one commanded by Colonel Alphonso F. Cook, the other led by Colonel William F. Morgan.

Rosser led his small force out of Staunton on January 7, on icy roads through high snowdrifts. On the night of January 10 the shivering raiders bivouacked on a mountainside near a road intersection of the Phillipi Turnpike, north of their objective. Before dawn most of the raiders advanced dismounted on the hardpacked snow. A smaller mounted element galloped ahead into the sleeping encampments of the 8th and 34th Ohio Infantry Regiments. A very few of the blue infantry struggled out of their tents and offered token resistance, but most of them quietly surrendered. Six Federals were killed and 32 were wounded. The Confederates had one killed and a few wounded, including Colonel Cook.

Rosser captured 100 good horses, 600 new weapons and accouterments, and 10,000 rations. His men ate as much as they could and retired back to Staunton with the remaining rations that would keep them fed for several more weeks.

General Rosser refused to surrender at Appomattox but took his parole the following month, and subsequently became quite wealthy as chief engineer of the Northern Pacific and Canadian Pacific Railroads. Rosser wore the blue uniform of a U.S. brigadier general in the Spanish-American War in 1898.

Below: **Rosser had been promoted to brigadier general in September 1863 and brilliantly led the Laurel Brigade against his old friend George Custer, but was unable to end the Union occupation of much of the valley. This sketch by A. R. Waud depicts Confederate cavalry under Rosser attacking the Federal rear near Harrisonburg, Virginia, in the Shenandoah Valley, on October 8, 1864. Just weeks later he began his successful raids into West Virginia.**

Damage caused by the English-built raider CSS *Alabama* became the core of an international dispute between the United States and England that was not settled until 1872 by extensive arbitration before a tribunal in Geneva, Switzerland. Under the command of fearless raider Raphael Semmes, *Alabama* was finally sunk in international waters off Cherbourg, France, on June 19, 1864. This view of her was painted by RADM J. W. Schmidt, USN, Ret., in 1961.

RAIDS ON WATER

The unprecedented advances in marine design, propulsion and armament in the mid-19th century changed the face of maritime warfare forever. The days of iron men and wooden ships were gone and the almost overnight transition to steam-powered, screw-driven, armored, steel-hulled ships armed with long-range rifled cannon and torpedoes presented new and exciting opportunities for heretofore unimaginable riverine and maritime raiding operations.

At the outset of hostilities, the Union Navy was far superior to that of the Confederate states, in reality and on paper. Some Federal ships were on foreign stations, far from the seat of the war and others were obsolescent or not even in service but laid up in yards. Nevertheless, the Union Navy existed and had a trained body of men.

The Confederate Navy was up against almost insurmountable odds, including no ships and insufficient funds and material with which to build them. Faced with such daunting difficulties the fledgling service was forced to think outside existing naval doctrine and seek unconventional means to offset these disadvantages. The brilliant results were the development of light, fast commerce raiders, a superior class of armored rams, torpedo boats and submarines, and mines and torpedoes.

The Civil War fostered advances and innovations that suddenly began to make the world a much smaller place and heralded new awareness among nations that distance and isolation were no longer a defense.

The Confederate High Seas Raiders

Right: Captain James Dunwoody Bulloch was the Confederate States naval agent in Europe appointed by Secretary of the Navy Stephen R. Mallory. Bulloch set up shop in Liverpool, England, in June 1861 and began implementing a fascinating three-point plan. Bulloch's concept was to buy or build fast commerce raiders to prey on commerce, state-of-the-art warships to break the blockade, and a fleet of blockade-runners to supply arms and munitions to the Confederate forces. In the face of incredible difficulties, he was remarkably successful in all three efforts.

Below: Bulloch faced the same difficulties getting *Florida* to sea as he did with *Alabama*. This ship left England as the *Oreto* and was armed and commissioned off Nassau by Captain J. N. Maffitt. After refitting at Mobile, *Florida* began her historic cruise. The Confederate raider is depicted capturing the *Jacob Bell*, valued at $1.5 million, reputedly the single most valuable prize taken during the war.

The main offensive strategy adopted by Confederate Secretary of the Navy Stephen R. Mallory, was the clandestine acquisition of commerce raiders, either by purchase or construction in England, and their use against the maritime fleet of the United States.

Mallory entrusted this mission to naval purchasing agent Commander James Dunwoody Bulloch, assisted by Commander James H. North. CSS *Florida* and CSS *Alabama* were built from the keel up on modified Royal Navy gunboat plans and became the two most famous and feared raiders of the war. Another steamer was bought and converted into CSS *Shenandoah*. While there were other vessels that did good service, these three ships accounted for 60 percent of the prizes taken during the four years of conflict.

The first of the famous raiders began her career as *Oreto* in the shipyards of Messrs. William C. Miller & Sons at Liverpool. Her engines were built by Fawcett, Preston & Company of that city. The finished vessel, a 192-foot, 700-ton, barque-rigged, steam-powered ship, was quietly paid for out of the Confederate Navy account at Fraser, Trenholm & Company, also of Liverpool. *Oreto* sailed from Liverpool on March 22, 1862, allegedly for

Sicily but actually for the Bahamas, where she met tenders at Green Cay. In mid-August 1862 she took on her armament of six 6-inch and two 7-inch Blakely rifles, at which time the ship was officially christened CSS *Florida* and John Newland Maffitt took command.

Florida sailed from Nassau into Mobile, Alabama, on September 4, 1862, for repairs and on January 17, 1863, left Mobile on her first cruise. She is credited with forty-seven prizes,

Left: CSS *Florida* was the first foreign-built raider to be commissioned as a vessel of the Confederate Navy. This photograph of the ship was probably made in the harbor at Brest, France, in 1863. Although her record did not equal that of the *Alabama*, both were feared, and countless ships of the Union Navy spent months searching the seas for the elusive raiders.

including those taken by Lieutenant Charles W. Read who used one prize as a cruiser and made additional captures. Badly in need of refitting, *Florida* put into Brest, France, on August 23 and remained there until February 10, 1864, when she sailed on her second cruise commanded by Lieutenant Charles M. Morris. She captured thirteen prizes before putting into the neutral port of Bahia, Brazil, on October 7, 1864, to refuel and refit. There, she was illegally captured by USS *Wachusett*, a Union steam sloop. Returned to the United States, *Florida* mysteriously sank at Hampton Roads. During her career *Florida* destroyed ships worth an estimated value of ten times her own cost.

One of *Florida*'s pivot guns, a 7-inch (100-pounder) Blakely rifle, made by Fawcett, Preston & Co., Liverpool, survives today at the Washington Navy Yard, and three of her flags taken in Brazil are preserved in the collections of the Civil War Library and Museum in Philadelphia.

CSS *Alabama* started life when construction of Hull Number 290 began at the Laird and Sons Birkenhead Ironworks on the River Mersey, across from Liverpool, in June 1861. The ship was 210 feet long with a beam of 32 feet, and her sleek wooden hull was designed for ease of repair in primitive port facilities. She was driven by steam propulsion engines and carried a full auxiliary sailing rig. She had a lifting screw mechanism that allowed the propeller to be lifted out of the water when under sail so as to extend her range.

Hull 290 was eventually christened *Enrica* and she sailed at dawn, July 29, 1862, one jump ahead of English authorities who were ordered to impound the vessel at the unrelenting insistence of U.S. Ambassador Charles Francis Adams. On her arrival at Terceira, in The Azores, armament was put aboard and Captain Raphael Semmes assumed command of the newly christened CSS *Alabama*. The fleet raider was "built for speed rather than

Left: The *Alabama* is shown in this sepia wash drawing by Clary Ray done in November 1894. In July 1861 Bulloch contracted with the Laird Shipyard in Birkenhead, on the Mersey River across from Liverpool, for the construction of this vessel initially known as *Hull 290*. U.S. authorities quickly realized who the real owners of the ship would be and invoked Queen Victoria's May 1861 Neutrality Proclamation in efforts to thwart Bulloch's plans. Eventually, the ship sailed under the name *Enrica* and was armed outside English waters and commissioned CSS *Alabama*. Raphael Semmes was her first captain.

Right: In this heroic painting by Maliby Sykes, Raphael Semmes wears the uniform of a rear admiral and carries the magnificent sword presented to him by friends in England after the sinking of the *Alabama*. Captain Semmes and Lieutenant Kell jumped into the sea as the ship sank and were picked up by the English yacht *Deerhound* and taken back to England. He returned to Mobile, Alabama, received a commission as an army brigadier general and commanded a naval brigade of sailors without ships at the end of the war, surrendering with Johnson's army in North Carolina.

Center: This engraving from an 1863 photograph made in Kingston, Jamaica, is probably a truer likeness of Semmes. His meticulously waxed mustache was one of his trademarks. Not only a seaman but a practicing attorney before the war, Semmes was forbidden to hold public office after the war and was under arrest for four months. He published his 833-page epic *Memoirs of Service Afloat During the War Between the States* in 1869.

Below right: The officers of USS *Kearsarge* gather on deck, one of the sequence of photographs made off Cherbourg. Captain John Ancrum Winslow stands third from left with thumb tucked in coat. The rings on the deck are the track that allows the huge pivot gun to go into action to either port or starboard. Semmes and Winslow had been messmates before the war aboard USS *Cumberland*.

battle" and was capable of just over 15 knots. Just in case she would meet much resistance, *Alabama* mounted eight guns, six 32-pounders in broadside and a 7-inch Blakely rifle and 6-inch smoothbore on pivot carriages amidships. The total cost of *Alabama* was $250,305.44.

Alabama operated around the Azores and then off Newfoundland before moving to the Gulf of Mexico. She went down the coast of Brazil and into the South Atlantic, and around the tip of Africa into the Indian Ocean, before retracing her route, re-crossing the South Atlantic and putting into Cherbourg, France, for badly need repairs. She was sunk off Cherbourg by the steam sloop, USS *Kearsarge*, on the morning of June 19, 1864.

By that time CSS *Alabama* had captured or destroyed sixty-nine Union ships valued at $7,000,000 during a twenty-two-month career. She had the distinction of being the only Confederate ship to sink a Federal warship, USS *Hatteras*, on the high seas. England paid 15.5 million dollars in damages to the United States in 1872 to settle claims against the English-built ship.

The *Alabama* was discovered by French military divers in 1984 seven nautical miles off Cherbourg in 198 feet of water. The CSS Alabama Association, assisted by a Franco-American alliance, is involved in ongoing documentation of the site and, since 1988, has recovered numerous relics. Artifacts include the ship's bell recovered in 2002 and all cannon including the 7-inch Blakely rifle and carriage. The ship's bell was sent to the Warren Lasch Archaeological Conservation in Charleston for conservation. In September 2004 the Civil War Trust named Cherbourg a Civil War Historic Site, the first site outside the United States. One of the recovered cannon is on loan to the Cité de le Mer Museum in that city. There are over 4,000 Web sites on the Internet dedicated to just this sea raider, indicative of the enormous interest in the topic.

The *Sea King*, a fast 220-foot steam-auxiliary cruiser, was purchased by the Confederates in

Left: Confederate naval officers Lieutenants Richard Armstrong, left, and Arthur Sinclair stand next to one of *Alabama*'s 32-pounder broadside guns. Both officers appear to wear the regulation Confederate naval uniform. The photograph was taken during a coaling stop, either at Cape Town or Luanda.

Center: Lieutenant John McIntosh Kell served most of his Confederate naval career under Semmes and became a close personal confidant. He was a loyal and efficient officer and rarely left the *Alabama* during her long cruise. He commanded the ironclad *Richmond* of the James River fleet after returning to the Confederacy.

Center right: William Smith was gun captain of the aft 11-inch Dahlgren pivot gun of USS *Kearsarge.* Battle reports indicate that the Union gun crew's proficiency was noteworthy. Marksmanship was exceptional and this gun reputedly did most of the damage to *Alabama* in the historic fight off Cherbourg, France.

Below left: The local French photographer Rondln made some wonderful photographs aboard *Kearsarge* at Cherbourg. Acting Master James R. Wheeler, left, and Assistant Engineer Sidney L. Smith stand next to the forward Dahlgren pivot gun. Projectiles for the gun stand on the deck. The first object may actually be a tompion or wad, then shell and grape.

Above: This painting done by artist J. O. Davidson in 1887 depicts the cheering Union crew of one of the pivot guns as the *Alabama* begins to settle by the stern. Federal gun crews kept up firing after the Confederate flag was lowered. Captain Winslow of *Kearsarge* stated after the battle that he continued firing because Semmes could not be trusted. When a white flag was raised Union gun crews ceased firing.

Right: The deck of *Alabama* was littered with dead and wounded, and all of the small boats were damaged to some degree. Semmes sent some wounded to *Kearsarge* in one boat and requested all aid and assistance. The Federal captain evidently did not order his boats away with any urgency to board the sinking raider and, before Semmes and Kell jumped into the Channel, they threw their swords away rather than surrender them. Subsequently, there were rumors that Captain Winslow allowed Semmes to escape to England.

April 1864 and converted to commerce raider, with armament including two Whitworth 32-pounder rifles that were put aboard at Madeira, Europe. She met the supply ship *Laurel* a week out of Liverpool in the Bay of Funchal, near Loo Rock, transferred arms, and was commissioned CSS *Shenandoah* on October 19, 1864, with James Iredell Waddell in command. This vessel was the only Confederate ship to circumnavigate the globe, on a 58,000-mile cruise, visiting Aus-

tralia, the Caroline islands, the Sea of Japan and the Arctic Ocean while destroying a large portion of the U.S. Pacific whaling fleet in the Bering Sea between Siberia and Alaska.

Waddell learned that the war was over in August 1865 and sailed for England, where the ship was interned on November 6, 1865, the last vessel to fly the Confederate flag. CSS *Shenandoah* captured thirty-eight prizes valued at $1,172,233 during her short career. Sold by

England to the Sultan of Zanzibar, she reportedly sank on a reef in the northern Indian Ocean in 1878.

The devastation of the U. S. maritime fleet was a catastrophe. Direct damage caused by the Confederate raiders has been estimated at between $15,000,000 and $25,000,000, and represents a loss of about 200 ships actually destroyed by the raiders. Furthermore, for every vessel destroyed, eight others were lost because of transfer to other flags to avoid exorbitant insurance rates. Indirect damage caused by the cruisers cannot be accurately estimated because of so many intangibles. It cost the United States $3,325,000 in operations just to search for the Rebel raiders. The burning of fishing and whaling fleets, and the coastal

raids, caused pandemonium along the entire East Coast. Only when one totals the damage does the real significance of Confederate cruisers become apparent. The American flag was almost swept from the seas, a blow from which the United States merchant service did not recover until 1918. If the Confederacy had done

Above: CSS *Shenandoah* was under the able command of Lieutenant James I. Waddell. *Shenandoah* destroyed much of the U.S. whaling fleet, the majority of it after the war. The ship is shown steaming through scattered ice in the Arctic Ocean in search of prey. When Waddell confirmed that the war was over, he disarmed his ship and sailed for Liverpool and internment.

Above left: CSS *Shenandoah* underwent repairs and refitting in Melbourne, Australia, in February 1865. The constant maintenance on wooden hulled ships was daunting and Confederate vessels did not enjoy the luxury of the courtesy of every port. Here the ship has been hauled out of water at the Williamstown Dockyard. In most cases repairs were make-do at sea.

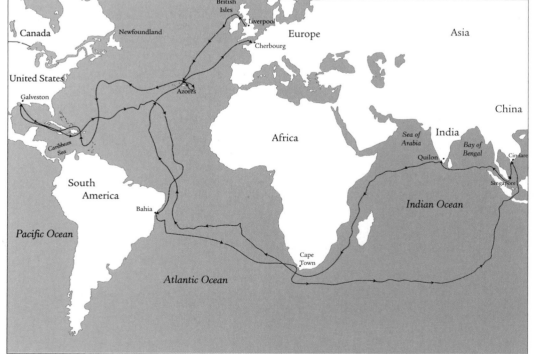

Left: Voyages of CSS *Alabama*.

one-tenth as well in other areas, she might have won the war.

The Blockade-runners

Life in the South was based on an agrarian economy and the area lacked the technology and raw materials to develop any meaningful industrial capacity. Prior to the Civil War almost all manufactured goods were purchased from the industrialized North. With the outbreak of hostilities, this source was no longer available. The new Confederacy was forced to look to Europe for basic necessities, even down to needles and thread. The most critical needs were arms and equipment with which to fight the war. The survival of the Confederacy absolutely depended on importation of critical military supplies.

On April 16, 1861, President Lincoln imposed a blockade on nearly 3,500 miles of coastline including the primary ports of Galveston, New Orleans, Mobile, Savannah, Charleston and Wilmington, to isolate the Confederacy and deprive her of the ability to import munitions of war. While the blockade got off to a slow start because of lack of available vessels, the Federal Navy grew rapidly by construction and purchase. By January 1865 it had over 470 vessels on blockade duty.

To combat this economic strangulation, the Confederate government and private business interests developed a new class of ship, the blockade-runner. Initially, arms and equipment and other material purchased in England were shipped on vessels directly to Southern ports. Very quickly it became apparent that the blockade was a reality and that these larger, slower ships were inadequate for the task. A more reliable and efficient system was developed. Confederate ordnance stations were established at Havana, Cuba, Nassau, New Providence and St. George, Bermuda. Ordnance shipments were brought by transatlantic steamers to these neutral English ports, where cargoes were off-loaded into warehouses leased by Confederate agents. The bulk shipments were broken down into smaller consignments, called trans-shipment or breaking bulk, and loaded on swift blockade-runners for the short three-day run to various Confederate ports. By mid-1863 sophisticated, purpose-built ships were performing this task.

The purpose-built blockade-runner was a streamlined, shallow draft vessel that has been called the first stealth craft. Most had a long, slender hull, a rounded stern to reduce wake, and a graceful bow to keep the prow low in the water and minimize bow wave. Since the bow was designed to knife through the sea rather than ride over it, the forecastle was covered by a convex metal overhead called a "turtleback" to deflect water off the deck. Many were iron-framed, steam-powered ships with metal hulls and even some degree of watertight compartmentalization. Ideally, these ships were about 170 feet in length with a beam of around 30 feet, and with cargo holds forward and aft of a central engine area. Two powerful but compact engines, mounted as low in the hull as engineering would allow, driving either screws or side-wheels, usually propelled this type of ship. In an effort to decrease sound, steam was vented underwater, and those driven by paddlewheels often had canvas sound abatement curtains hung over paddleboxes. Most had an extremely low freeboard, abbreviated or skeletonized superstructure, raked or hinged masts, telescoping funnels – anything to minimize their silhouette. The runner was usually

Below right: Blockade-runners often had many careers. Originally *Giraffe*, built in Scotland, this ship was renamed *R. E. Lee* when she was bought by the Confederacy in December 1862. Captured by the blockader James Adger near Beaufort, adjudicated in prize court and purchased by the U.S. Navy, she became USS *Fort Donelson*, shown here off Norfolk, Virginia, in December 1864. After the war she was sold to private interests and became *Isabella*.

Bottom right: The wheels and paddle boxes are still visible in the photograph of this wreck of the blockade-runner *Colt* off Sullivan's Island, just north of Charleston, taken in 1865. The port of Charleston saw the arrival of more than one hundred blockade-runners during the war, some multiple trips by the same ship, some so regular as to run on schedule. The tonnage of supplies and equipment brought into the Confederacy in these ships was astounding.

Left: Bat, built by Jones, Quiggin & Company, Liverpool, in 1864 for the Confederate firm of Fraser, Trenholm & Company, was captured by USS *Montgomery* trying to reach Old Inlet near Wilmington on October 8, 1864, and shown here off Fort Monroe. The vessel was sold after the war in November 1865 to private interests and became *Teazer.* The turtleback forecastle, raked stacks and lead-colored paint scheme make this a great example of a late war purpose-built blockade-runner.

painted a pale color, a light gray or dirty white, the first recognized use of naval camouflage.

The captain and crew of such a ship were an adventuresome lot. Unquestionably, some were patriotic, but the very generous compensation and lucrative opportunities were often the primary incentives. The captain might receive the equivalent of $5,000 in gold for a successful trip, chief engineers and pilots $2,500, and even ordinary seamen $250 – at least ten or even twenty times the pay of regular seamen. Profits of 1,100 percent on small luxury items were not uncommon. The pay was commensurate with dangers faced.

In situations of extreme duress captains would resort to burning cotton soaked with turpentine or even sides of bacon for fuel to maximize speed. Sometimes runners attained speeds of nearly 15 knots, racing through shoal waters on a pitch black night or in blinding rain. Sweating, frantic crewmembers stoked the pounding engines and a leadsman continually checked water depth as pursuing blockaders closed in from all sides, lofting flares for illumination and throwing large-caliber shells at them. Not an occupation for the faint of heart.

Union blockading ships were loath to sink Confederate blockade-runners, and a lack of patriotism had nothing to do with it. The motivation was greed. The captain and crew of every Union ship that participated in the capture of a blockade-runner stood to profit handsomely when the ship and its cargo were sold at auction after prize court adjudication. The captain and crew received one-half the proceeds split on a scale dependent upon rank. Therefore, great effort was made to capture these runners and they were destroyed only as a last resort. Several senior officers ended the war quite wealthy due to this practice.

The first blockade-runner, *Bermuda,* sailed with a major cargo of ordnance from Liverpool on August 22, 1861, directly to Savannah, Georgia, arriving on September 17. *Banshee* was the first steel-hulled side-wheeler to cross the Atlantic and was built by Jones, Quiggan & Co., in Liverpool. She was privately owned by the Anglo-Confederate Trading Company and made fourteen successful roundtrips. *Hattie* probably holds the record with some sixty trips, some of them in broad daylight. Of 350 known blockade-runners, some 225, the great majority, were built in England.

The capture of Ft. Fisher and the loss of the port of Wilmington early in 1865 heralded the end of blockade running, leaving literally tons of material lying in Bermuda, Nassau and Cuba. The lifeline of the Confederacy had been cut.

During the war at least 1,300 attempts were made to run the blockade. Probably 1,000 of these attempts were successful. The Union fleets captured 136 ships and destroyed 85, although the cargoes of some of the latter were salvaged in part. The tonnage of supplies brought through the blockade is unknown but it was enormous, and over 400,000 bales of cotton were taken out to England. The efforts of these daring men and their beautiful, fragile ships enabled the Confederacy to exist, and when they could no longer carry that burden, the war ended.

Ellet Captures Memphis

Below: Secretary of War Stanton authorized Ellet to purchase nine decrepit steamboats and modify them to rams according to his own specifications. This was done by stacking cotton bales around propulsion units and reinforcing strategic components of the old vessels. *Monarch* is in the foreground flanked by *Queen of the West, Lioness, Switzerland* and *T. D. Horner*.

Right: This illustration, after a sketch by Rear-Admiral Walke, depicts the remains of the Confederate fleet retreating downriver with the Federal ironclads in the background. Whatever battle plan Captain James E. Montgomery had for his Confederate River Defense Fleet disintegrated when Ellet's *Queen of the West* steamed at 20 knots into the Confederate fleet, disrupting any semblance of order.

A startling riverine force made its debut under army command during the catastrophic event known as the naval battle of Memphis in June 1862. This waterborne weapons system was the brainchild of Federal Colonel Charles Ellet and was endorsed by Secretary of War Edwin M. Stanton. Ellet purchased worn out steamboats and reinforced the hulls and bows with heavy timbers and built protective bulkheads around the propulsion unit. Skeleton crews manned the unarmed ships. Colonel Ellet said, "The boats I have purchased are illy [sic] adapted for the work I shall require of them; it is not their strength upon which I rely, but upon the audacity of our attack." The basic premise was that the ships were expendable and their sole offensive use was to ram or run down opposing vessels – not particularly sophisticated but frighteningly effective.

Ellet's objective was Memphis, the second largest and fastest growing city in the state of Tennessee, with a population over 22,000 in 1861. An important river port, rail center and cotton market, it had earlier been the site of shipbuilding and ordnance activity. But, by June 1862, the strategic town was defended only by a "make do" fleet of eight converted and inadequately armed riverboats and a few local troops under the command of Brigadier General M. Jeff Thompson.

Union Admiral Andrew H. Foote, USN, commanded Union naval forces on the Mississippi River. Reporting to Foote was Captain Charles H. Davis, USN, commanding five Eads-built City Class ironclads, *Benton, Cairo, Carondolet, Louisville* and *St. Louis.* Somewhat

under the command of Captain Davis but beholden to Secretary of War Stanton was army Colonel Ellet with his steam rams, *Queen of the West*, *Monarch* and several others, a byzantine chain of command.

Inter-service rivalries aside, Foote saw this as a great opportunity to run down the river and take the weakly defended city. The Federal ships, nominally under Davis, anchored above Memphis, the ironclads in a line across the river. Early on the morning of June 6, 1862, the Federal fleet challenged the Confederate ships in front of the city and the civilian population lined the bluff overlooking the river to watch the battle.

The Confederate River Defense Fleet, commanded by Captain James E. Montgomery, consisted of *General Beauregard*, *General Bragg*, *General Van Dorn*, *General Thompson*, *Colonel Lovell*, *Sumter* and *Little Rebel*, lightly armed and armored steamboats. They moved upriver and initiated the contest. The Federal ironclads answered as the steam rams gathered on the Arkansas side of the river. Suddenly, upon hearing the first gun, Ellet ordered his ram, *Queen of the West*, to proceed full speed head-on at the bow of *General Lovell* in the center of the advancing Confederate line. At the same time he directed *Monarch* to ram *General Price*. As the ram rapidly closed Ellet stood forward on the hurricane deck. The captain of *General Lovell* lost his nerve at the last minute and turned to avoid a head-on collision, allowing the Union ship to strike amidships, cutting the Confederate vessel almost in two and sinking her immediately. *General Price*, in a frantic effort to avoid

Monarch, turned and had her starboard wheel accidentally sheared off by *General Beauregard*.

Ellet's *Queen of the West* then engaged both *Beauregard* and *Sumter* on either side of her. By now Ellet was lying on the deck with a pistol ball in his leg, but still in command. The sinking *General Price* beached on the Arkansas side pursued by the disabled *Star of the West*, and *Little Rebel* ran aground in the swirling melee. *Jeff Thompson* was set afire by her abandoning crew and disintegrated in an enormous detonation. In just about an hour the Southern ships were captured, sunk, burned or run aground. *Van Dorn* escaped downriver, only to be burned later.

Colonel Ellet sent his son, Medical Cadet Lieutenant Charles R. Ellet, ashore, to demand surrender of the city, but Captain Davis, USN, accepted the surrender from the stunned mayor around 11:00 AM. Ironically, the only Union casualty was Colonel Ellet, who was mortally wounded and died June 21. Colonel Ellet was given a state funeral at Independence Hall in Philadelphia. Smacking a little of nepotism, his brother, army Brigadier General Alfred W. Ellet, assumed command of the rams.

Below, inset: Medical Cadet Charles Rivers Ellet, in the uniform of an infantry colonel, served under his father, Charles Ellet, Jr., who was best known as an engineer and master builder of suspension bridges rather than an army commander of a river fleet. Young Ellet was the first Federal officer to enter Memphis. The senior Ellet, who was born in 1810, developed his concept of ram boats as an observer during the Crimean War.

Bottom left: The population of Memphis gathered on the bluff overlooking the Mississippi to witness the battle. The disaster was over almost before it started. Wounded Colonel Ellet sent his son, a nineteen-year-old Medical Cadet aboard *Lioness*, to accept the surrender of the town, to the displeasure of Captain Davis, USN, who assumed the honor as ranking officer.

Below: Young Cadet Ellet and three marines went ashore in a small boat under a flag of truce and, although faced by a large and threatening crowd, marched to the Post Office, lowered the Confederate flag and replaced it with the U.S. flag. Federal troops under Colonel G. N. Fitch occupied the town later in the afternoon.

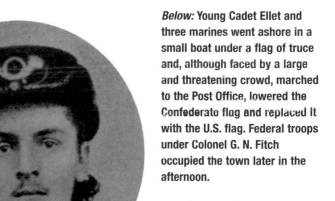

Wood – Extraordinary Naval Commando

Below left: Wood's raiders not only used special boats but also special equipment and identification devices. He described the armament of the assault parties as consisting of "nine-shot French revolvers and cutlasses." Wood was referring to the massive nine-shot .42-caliber LeMat Revolver which also had a shotgun barrel that served as the cylinder pin. The discharge of this barrel would be most effective in any boarding operation. His men also wore distinctive sleeve bands or brassards so that friend could be identified from foe in night actions.

Below right: This engraving of John Taylor Wood was made from a photograph taken in Canada in 1867. Wood accompanied the presidential party during the flight south at the end of the war. He managed to escape Federal capture in Georgia and sailed to Cuba in a small open boat rather than surrender, a feat no less unusual than any other of his daring adventures. He never returned to the South but spent the rest of his life in Halifax, Nova Scotia.

John Taylor Wood, Naval Academy, Class of 1853, was one of a small group of brilliant military minds that generated covert operations during the Civil War that were equal to any modern day high-tech military adventure. Wood may be considered one of the fathers of the brown water navy, a 19th century equivalent of the PCF (Patrol Craft Fast) or Swift boat commander, an early advocate of special weapons and tactics. He was aggressive, innovative and focused, and his family connections made him adept at cutting through bureaucratic military red tape. He was a grandson of President Zachary Taylor, son of Major, later General, Robert Crooke Wood, U.S. Army, and nephew of both Confederate President Jefferson Davis and Lieutenant General Richard Taylor of Louisiana. His brother, Colonel Robert C. Wood, Jr., West Point, rode under General John Hunt Morgan.

In 1861, Wood was an instructor in naval gunnery and tactics at the Naval Academy but quickly cast his lot with the fledgling Confederate Navy. He commanded the forward pivot gun on CSS *Virginia* against USS *Monitor* in the historic first battle between ironclads at Hampton Roads. His genius and potential were recognized and Jefferson Davis appointed him his naval aide. Wood eventually held the dual rank of colonel of cavalry in the army and commander in the navy, a most unusual situation.

Wood's fertile mind conceived the idea of taking the war to the enemy by transporting small craft overland on specially modified wagon chassis to rivers or estuaries behind enemy lines, and launching the craft for night assaults on an unsuspecting foe. These unusual tactics earned the appellations of "navy on wheels" and "amphibious horse marines" for his special force.

The concept was enthusiastically approved and Wood received funding to proceed with the project. He developed a modified design of whaleboat with storage space for arms, ammunition, special equipment and supplies for a week of extended operations. The light, shallow-draft boats were built at Rocketts Navy Yard on the north bank of the James River, just below Richmond. The boats were manned by specially selected crews of ten to twenty men trained in boarding tactics and commanded by an officer, all armed with LeMat revolvers, cutlasses and boarding axes, and supported by a small marine complement armed with Enfield rifles. The assault parties all wore white armbands on their left sleeves so that each could be recognized during the assault.

The plan was to row up to an unsuspecting enemy craft, with muffled oars in absolute silence, throw grapnels over the anti-boarding nets of the target and storm the vessel. The boarding party would climb the nets while the marines still in the launches engaged any de-

fenders who showed themselves. Wood even specified the capture of the forward section of the target ship first so as to prevent the crew from slipping anchor and escaping. Once in control, the raiders had the option to burn the capture or turn it into a privateer.

Wood led a number of successful overland raids against Federal ships, but perhaps his most daring was the assault and capture of USS *Underwriter* as part of a combined water and land operation to capture New Berne, North Carolina, in 1864. His was a supporting role, the only successful part of an abortive raid, but as usual his execution was flawless.

Wood led fourteen cutters each manned by ten men and two officers down the Neuse River on the afternoon of February 1. The assault party stopped above the target at dark and finalized their operational plan. *Underwriter*, a heavy converted seagoing tugboat, the largest gunboat at New Berne, was 186 feet long, mounted two big 8-inch guns and other smaller ordnance, and had a crew of eighty-four officers and men.

The Confederates approached in a double line and, when the first Union lookout shouted the alarm, all hands rowed hard to both sides of the ship and the assault parties boarded. The melee of brutal hand-to-hand night combat was over in minutes. Confederate losses were six killed and twenty-two wounded. Federal losses were nine killed, including the commanding officer, and twenty wounded, all of whom were removed at

Wood's orders before the ship was destroyed. Twenty-six of the Union forces were taken prisoner and twenty-three escaped. John Taylor Wood formally received the Thanks of the Confederate Congress for this action.

In August 1864 Wood became a deep-water sailor and commanded the raider CSS *Tallahassie*. During a three-week rampage along the Atlantic coast from New York to Maine, he captured or destroyed thirty-one Northern fishing and coastal vessels and put the northeast into a state of panic. Wood's activities greatly embarrassed Union forces and caused thousands of troops to be withheld from combat theaters to guard against a possible foray into New York harbor.

At the war's end, Wood accompanied the presidential party in the attempt to escape and evade Federal forces. Wood eventually made his way to Cuba in June 1865 and later settled in Halifax, Nova Scotia, where he died in 1904. After the war he wrote articles for *Century Magazine* and assisted Jefferson Davis in writing his two-volume memoirs. One of his faithful lieutenants, J. Thomas Scharf, wrote the authoritative *History of the Confederate States Navy*, in 1894.

John Taylor Wood was recognized even during the war as the South's most successful maritime raider, and his escapades raised flagging Southern morale on several occasions. He ranked only second to Raphael Semmes in the number of prizes taken during his career.

Below: Wood quickly recognized the obvious supremacy of the Federal Navy but he realized that unexpected, clandestine operations could damage the much stronger foe. He relied on the old naval tactic known as a cutting-out expedition with modifications of his own to accomplish this end. Wood adapted wagon frames to carry modified open cutters overland at night to launch against unsuspecting Federal shipping in rivers and estuaries. His efforts were quite successful and of great propaganda value. The destruction of the *Underwriter* at New Berne was one of his more notable victories.

The First Torpedo Boats

Below: This *David*-class vessel, lying beside a bulkhead near Charleston, still has the smokestack in place forward of the crew space and the spar torpedo boom afixed to the bow. The screw at the stern is evidently damaged. The wagon in front of the house is that of the photographer who made this image.

The prototype *David* "submarine" was built in Charleston in 1863 by a civilian consortium including David Ebaugh and Theodore Stoney known as the Southern Torpedo Company. The cigar-shaped craft was not a true submarine but actually a semi-submersible powered by a conventional steam engine. The design was successful enough to produce a class of vessels of which an estimated twelve to fourteen were built in at least three locations. Boats of this type participated in several attempts to break the blockade.

The first boat was fifty feet long with a six-foot beam and five-foot draft. It was armed with a torpedo containing at least fifty pounds of black powder, mounted on a ten-foot-long spar. The engine, mounted forward of the crew compartment in the bow, powered the boat at 5-7 knots. The hulls of the boats were all wood, although some were partially sheathed in iron plate for protection against small arms fire and the concussive force from the detonation of the torpedo.

The spar torpedo was mounted on the bow of the boat and fitted with a sharp, barbed head that was intended to punch into the wooden hull of the target vessel below the water line. The torpedo boat would then reverse course, leaving the torpedo embedded in the hull of the ship. At a safe distance the torpedo-man would detonate the torpedo by pulling a long lanyard that would activate the firing mechanism of the weapon. This type of torpedo was used on other vessels, including the submarine CSS *Hunley*.

The USS *New Ironsides*, built by Merrick & Sons in Philadelphia and launched in 1862, was Admiral Samuel F. Du Pont's flagship of the South Atlantic Blockading Squadron. She

was a powerful, 3,486-ton steam frigate. Nearly three-fourths of the 230-foot hull was covered with four-and-a-half-inch-thick iron-armored plate. The sixteen 11-inch Dahlgren guns were mounted in standard broadside configuration, eight to starboard and eight to port, the pride of the blockading fleet. In the eyes of many Southerners, *New Ironsides* was the despised symbol of the hated blockade. George Alfred Trenholm, senior partner of the Charleston importing and exporting firm of John Fraser & Company, posted a bounty of $100,000 payable to anyone who could sink *New Ironsides* or sister ship *Wabash* and $50,000 each for every Monitor-class vessel sunk.

Lieutenant William T. Glassell commanded *Little David* on October 5, 1863, and his aim was to sink the Union frigate. Engineer James H. Tomb manned the engine, seaman James Sullivan handled the weapon, and Walker Cannon was pilot. About 9:00 PM on that hazy evening *David* was 300 yards from the target anchored off Charleston, making for the unarmored starboard quarter of the hull, when she was sighted by an alert lookout. The Confederate vessel was hailed as she closed. Glassell did not answer but fired a shotgun, mortally wounding acting master Howard on the Federal ship, and proceeded to carefully place the spar torpedo, prior to a lanyard being pulled to detonate the charge. When the torpedo exploded the smaller craft heaved upward, and cascading water doused the flames in the little torpedo boat's boiler. With the boat dead in the water and marines aboard *New Ironsides* pelting the craft with musketry, Glassell ordered the crew to abandon ship.

Glassell and torpedo-man Sullivan were captured, and later the Confederate lieutenant was turned over to the Federal Admiral Dahlgren. Engineer Tomb and Cannon, the pilot, re-boarded the boat after she had drifted away from the frigate, got up steam and cruised back to Charleston where they arrived the next morning. The little craft had thirteen bullet holes in it from small arms fire from *New Ironsides*.

The official Federal account of the raid said, "…it was a failure and most of the rebels were taken prisoner, the rest were drowned; the *Ironsides* was not hurt, and only one man killed." In reality, the attack put senior naval officers almost in a state of panic, just what the Confederates intended. Admiral Dahlgren was so perturbed that he ordered fenders rigged around all ironclads with weighted nets hung from them for protection against torpedo attacks. He also offered a reward of up to $30,000 for the capture or destruction of any of these unconventional Rebel weapons.

Below: This example of a *David*-class vessel appears considerably longer than other boats of the class, evidently the result of ongoing modification and improvement. Most *Davids* had a crew of four. Armament was one spar torpedo with 100- to 150-pound explosive charge mounted on a 10-foot boom.

Right: USS *New Ironsides* was built in Philadelphia by Merrick & Sons and launched in May 1862, one of three experimental ironclad types. This painting by Clary Ray depicts the armored behemoth under full sail and steam. *New Ironsides* was the only vessel of this configuration built and was obsolete by the end of the war.

Above: At the end of the war the Charleston waterfront seemed to be littered with *David*-class semi-submersible boats. This one lying in front of a bulkhead close to one of the very fashionable and undamaged houses seems to have a higher than usual crew compartment freeboard. The smokestack for the steam engine is not present.

Although the Federal ship was able to remain on station until May 1864, she was, in fact, severely damaged and went back to Philadelphia for extensive repairs and refitting. The Confederates were elated by the partial success and began to build other similar craft, including one much larger boat, "Number Six," that was reportedly a hundred and sixty feet long.

Subsequently, Tomb was placed in command of the vessel and in March and April 1864 he led attacks against USS *Memphis* and USS *Wabash* off Charleston. Although these attacks were unsuccessful, and no damage resulted, the Federals' fear of underwater attack became an increasingly serious psychological weapon, almost an obsession, leading to the development of more elaborate torpedo booms and nets around Union ships in the blockading fleet. So pervading was the Union fear of these boats that at least ten more were started by the Confederates in Charleston, including *Torch* and *Midge*.

At the same time, CSS *Hunley*, a real submarine, was undergoing trials in the waters around Charleston. The boat had a restricted operational area because it was manually powered. At one point, when there were plans to attack shipping far out from *Hunley*'s base, *David* was detailed to increase the submarine's operational limits by towing her close to the attack position, thereby preserving the limited physical energy of the crew.

Other vessels of this class were built on the James River at Richmond following standard David configuration. These included *Hornet*, *Scorpion*, *Squib* and *Wasp*. Lieutenant Hunter Davidson, who established the Naval Submarine Battery Service, commanded *Squib*. On the night of April 9, 1864, he cruised through the whole Union fleet at Newport News and attacked the flagship USS *Minnesota*. He detonated a spar torpedo against the side of the ship, but too near the surface to do serious damage, and took his craft safely back up the James River. For his effort he was promoted to the rank of commander "for gallant and meritorious conduct."

Another *David*-class boat, *St. Patrick*, built at Selma Naval Ordnance Works, cruised in Mobile Bay and was a source of great concern to the blockading ships there. *Viper*, yet another *David*-class boat, built at the Columbus Naval Iron Works in Georgia, was operational in 1865. Evidently several of these boats were seized at the end of the war. *Midge* was taken to the Brooklyn Naval Yard for examination, and another was to be taken to the Naval Academy at Annapolis for study in the late 1860s.

The *David*-class boats did not earn the notoriety or historical importance of the *Hunley* because they never achieved the electrifying success of the first submarine. Nevertheless, these first primitive torpedo boats were certainly antecedents of the Motor Torpedo Boats (MTBs) and German *Schnellboots* (Fast Boats) of World War II, and were an important step in the evolution of naval warfare.

Above: This large semi-submersible, unidentified, possibly *David*-class craft, is moored between two Monitor-class vessels in a shipyard at the end of the war. The ventilators or cowl vents protruding from the deck are indicative of a larger vessel than the standard *Davids*. Possibly this was boat "Number Six."

Left: Another *David*-class boat was taken to the Naval Academy at Annapolis for testing and evaluation after the war. This example is moored with smokestack dismounted and laid horizontal for some reason. Admiral Dahlgren stated he saw at least nine *David*-class boats at Charleston at the end of the war.

Hunley Sinks the *Housatonic*

Right: James R. McClintock, one of the brains in the original development of the project, was involved in all three boats built by the group, *Pioneer*, *Pioneer II*, also known as *American Diver*, and *Hunley*. An electromagnetic engine was one method of propulsion that was considered but lack of material and dwindling resources forced the men to resort finally to manpower for propulsion of the craft.

Center: Horace Lawson Hunley and his partners designed and built *Pioneer* with private funds at New Orleans. They expected the vessel to become a licensed privateer and planned to recoup their investment by sinking Union vessels for which they would earn a bounty of 20 percent of the vessels' value. Federal forces occupied the city before the entrepreneurs could implement their plan.

Below right: This vessel has been identified incorrectly as *Pioneer*, McClintock's first submarine. It was found near New Orleans and sat for some years at the State Home for Confederate Soldiers at Bayou St. Johns. The peculiar contraption was moved to the Louisiana State Museum in 1957. A drawing of Pioneer done by William Shock, engineer aboard USS *Pensacola*, shortly after the Federal occupation of New Orleans, depicts an entirely different configuration. Most recent research indicates that this vessel is yet another unidentified Confederate submarine craft.

Baxter Watson and James R. McClintock, maritime engineers, partnered with financiers Horace L. Hunley, Robert R. Barrow, H. J. Leovy and James K. Scott to build the first submarine boat, Hunley's Fish Fin Torpedo Boat, actually *Pioneer*, in New Orleans during the winter of 1861-1862. The craft, described as "an oversized cigar," was fabricated of quarter-inch thick plate at the Leeds Foundry on the corner of Fourcher and Delord Streets at the cost of $2,600. A crew of four men manned the thirty-foot-long vessel. When the city fell in the spring of 1862, *Pioneer* was scuttled in New Basin Canal, only to be recovered by Federal forces and sold for $43 as scrap early in 1868, an ignominious end for the revolutionary craft.

But the Southern group took their idea to Mobile and constructed a second submersible, *Pioneer II* or *American Diver*, in the shops of Park and Lyons on the corner of Water and State Streets. Horace Hunley footed the bill

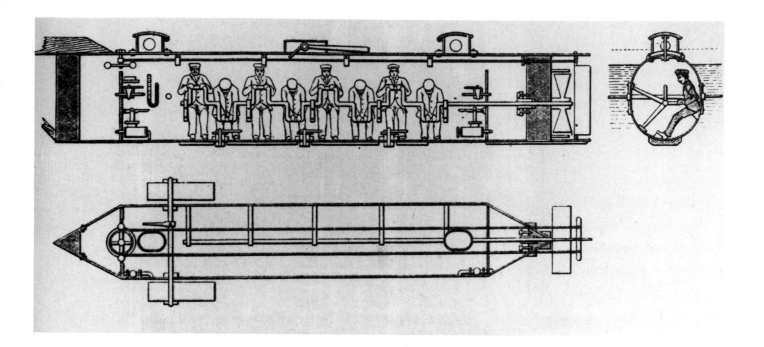

for the second boat. This craft was larger, thirty-six feet long, three feet wide and four feet high. The technologically improved boat operated in the bay during the winter of 1862-1863 but could only manage speeds of two miles an hour. A trial near Fort Morgan in February 1863 ended in disaster in the choppy waters of Mobile Bay. The crew managed to escape the sinking vessel, but it was lost and never recovered.

During the summer of 1863 a civilian group with a peculiar fascination for destructive devices, The Singer Submarine Corps, joined with Hunley's outfit to finance and construct a third submersible in Mobile, and the boat successfully sank a target barge in the bay. This craft was constructed using an old boiler, forty feet long overall with a claustrophobic ovoid crew space twenty-five feet long and just four feet high and three-and-a-half feet wide.

At the invitation of Confederate General P. G. T. Beauregard the vessel was transported overland by rail to Charleston in mid-August, with hopes that the secret weapon could break the blockade. General Thomas L. Clingman, commanding at Sullivan's Island, thought little of the civilian eggheads of Singer and placed the boat under military control within two weeks of arrival.

However, an accident occurred on August 29, 1863, as the boat sank almost at the dock. Four crewmen escaped, but five were drowned. Lieutenant Hasker was dragged 42 feet to the bottom, half out of the boat, before he managed to extricate his leg from a partially closed hatch and swim to the surface. Two veteran hard-hat divers, David Broadfoot and Angus Smith, raised the boat. After ten days on the bottom, the badly decomposed corpses were removed from the boat. The salvage team was forced to cut off some rigid limbs to squeeze the bodies through the narrow hatches, and the interior of the boat was cleaned with lime under Hunley's supervision. Shortly thereafter Hunley requested in writing to General Beauregard that the vessel revert to his control and the little boat soon became known as CSS *Hunley*. Lieutenant George E. Dixon came up from Mobile to command the boat.

Under Dixon the boat undertook a number of successful practice attacks against the ship CSS *Indian Chief*. The exercise involved the use of a towed torpedo on a 200-foot line trailing behind the sub. The craft dived under the target and pulled the device against the hull. On October 15, 1863, while Dixon was on leave, Hunley took his boat out at 9:25 AM for another training exercise. The inventor submerged the boat and never surfaced.

Divers Broadfoot and Smith were called again. When the boat was raised and the hatch was opened General Beauregard described the scene as "indescribably ghastly." The boat had been on the bottom for over three weeks and

Above: William A. Alexander's cut-away drawing of the interior of the submarine *H. L. Hunley* illustrates the crew positions within the little vessel. The drawing also shows the primitive controls and the snorkel system folded down on the center of the upper deck. The sterile drawing gives no inkling of the wet, cramped and suffocating conditions endured by the crew within the claustrophobic iron coffin.

Below: USS *Housatonic* was part of the Blockading Squadron laying siege to Charleston in early 1864. The siege operations had become a stalemate. The Union fleet couldn't take the city and the city refused to surrender. The officers and men of the Federal fleet were vaguely aware of the existence of Confederate undersea raiders but were ill-equipped and untrained in any methods to combat them. *Housatonic* was basically a sitting duck when *Hunley* struck.

the crew were "contorted into all kinds of horrible attitudes, some clutching candles, evidently endeavoring to force open the manholes; others lying in the bottom, tightly grappled together, and the blackened faces of all presented the expression of their despair and agony." The stiff, bloated corpses were most likely dismembered to remove them from the boat. The vessel that already was called "the peripatetic coffin" was soon called "the murdering machine." Normal, rational men would have called it a day, but new volunteers stepped forward even as the dead were dragged out of the boat. Hunley and his crew were buried in Magnolia Cemetery on November 8 and 9.

Lieutenant Dixon and eight brave souls took the bad-luck boat out against USS *Housatonic*, a 207-foot steam-powered screw sloop of war, on the calm, moonlit night of February 17, 1864. The Union ship was only three miles from the sub's base at Battery Marshall. The sub crept to within a few hundred yards of the Union vessel and surfaced for bearings. An alert Federal lookout saw something in the water and called the alarm. The

Hunley was already making her run and was too close for the ship's guns to bear, but some small arms fire was directed at her. The torpedo exploded on the starboard side of the Union vessel around 8:45 PM and the ship went down in minutes. *Housatonic* lost five dead and two injured. The submarine, which had become the first to sink a surface warship, was never seen again.

Oddly enough, while five of the crew were members of the navy when the submarine was sent out to attack the USS *Housatonic* in 1864, one of the great naval actions in history was ordered by an army general, P. G. T. Beauregard, and the vessel was commanded by an army officer, Lieutenant Dixon, who was never commissioned in the Confederate Navy. He was still a member of Company E, 21st Alabama Volunteer Infantry, when he and his crew went down in the *Hunley*. Second in command was Corporal C. F. Carlson, a member of Captain Wagener's German Light Artillery Company of South Carolina.

The *Hunley* was always assured of a place in naval history due to the incredible accom-

plishments of the vessel. An eight-foot-tall granite monument was raised at Battery Park in Charleston on May 8, 1899, and another monument was raised in Mobile, but that was just the beginning. A constant stream of publications concerning submarines, their progress and references to the *Hunley* appeared over the years, but the serious search for the vessel began only a quarter of a century ago. Action/adventure novelist Clive Cussler located the remains of *Housatonic* in 1980 and interest began to grow. *Hunley* was located on May 11, 1995, by a joint operation of Underwater Archaeology Division of the South Carolina Institute of Archaeology (SCIAA) and Cussler's National Underwater and Marine Agency (NUMA). The boat was raised on August 8, 2000, with extensive news coverage.

The story of the search for the vessel became a chapter in Cussler's only non-fiction book, *The Sea Hunters*, published in 1996. The *Hunley* is only one of more than sixty historically significant shipwrecks that form the basis for a project in the works for a nineteen-episode television series produced by Eco-Nova Productions, to be aired on the National Geographic Channel. The historic action was the subject of a movie *The Hunley*, in 1999, starring Armand Assante as Dixon and Donald Sutherland as General Beauregard. The *Hunley* was also a featured story in the July 2002 issue of *National Geographic*. The Friends of the Hunley have developed thehunley.com Web site and an online store, www.hunleystore.com, and also an online newsletter.

After the raising of the vessel, the remains of the final crewmen were re-interred with full military honors in Magnolia Cemetery on April 17, 2004, adjacent to the wartime graves of Horace Hunley and other crew members. The *Hunley* is presently undergoing comprehensive study and state-of-the-art preservation at the Warren Lasch Conservation Lab at the former Charleston Naval Base, in preparation for being a cornerstone of the new naval museum at Patriot's Point, along with the aircraft carrier *Yorktown*. The legacy of CSS *Hunley* grows daily and has actually spawned an industry.

Below: Hunley was photographed on the docks at Charleston after being raised again in early November 1863 and the bodies of Horace Hunley and his crew removed. The following month the submarine was the subject of a painting shown here by Conrad Wise Chapman. The aft hatch is still open, trying to ventilate the foul-smelling interior. The soldier leaning on the rudder gives some indication of the diminutive size of the vessel.

Beall's PoW Rescue Attempt

Right: **John Yates Beall, shown in a photograph made of him just hours before his execution, was unquestionably a duly commissioned Confederate officer. His execution in the waning days of the war is puzzling. It seems more an act of revenge rather than justice. His strategic concept of seizing the only formidable Union vessel on the Great Lakes and opening a second front seems far-fetched but, had he been successful, the results can only be imagined.**

John Yates Beall, like William Cushing and Charles Read, had personal access to senior members within the governments they served, either through family connections or social status. Often, such connections can greatly enhance one's career. In Beall's case, they proved fatal.

Beall (pronounced Bell) attended the University of Virginia and, before the war, served as a private in the Botts Greys, a local Virginia militia unit. He was present in the guard detail during John Brown's trial and befriended Corporal John Wilkes Booth, a member of the Richmond Grays, another militia unit. At the beginning of the war he joined Company G, 2nd Virginia Volunteers, was badly wounded at Harpers Ferry on October 16, 1861, and eventually discharged from service. Not fully recovered from his wounds, he volunteered for naval duty and was appointed an "acting master" of a privateer operating on Chesapeake Bay. He was known thereafter as Captain Beall. He had a flotilla consisting of two very small boats, the 22-foot *Raven* and 28-foot *Swan*, and about twenty men exempted from military service for various physical deficiencies. Nevertheless, the oversize rowboats and pesky invalids were the cause of considerable consternation to Federal forces around the bay.

Beall and several of his crew were captured November 14, 1863, put in irons and incarcerated at Fort McHenry at Baltimore, there to await trial as pirates, and certain execution. On behalf of Beall and his crew, Confederate Secretary of the Navy Mallory corresponded with Federal authorities, and advised that a like number of Union prisoners would face a similar fate. Beall's status was changed overnight from pirate to prisoner of war, and he was exchanged on May 5, 1864.

Back in Richmond, Beall visited President Davis and Secretary Mallory and proposed a plan for freeing prisoners at several prison camps, and opening a "second front" in the North. Secretary of War Seddon was impressed and offered Beall a lieutenant's commission in the Secret Service, but the young man refused because he did not want to be a spy. The idea of freeing prisoners of war at various locations intrigued several senior Confederates, and Beall found himself in Canada on August 14, 1864, reporting to Lieutenant Colonel Jacob Thompson, one of the commissioners in charge of Confederate operations there.

Beall's mission was to liberate the 3,200 Confederate officers confined in a sixteen-acre stockade surrounded by a fifteen-foot-

Below: This drawing of the U. S. Military Prison at Johnson's Island depicts sentries patrolling the walls of the stockade, the parade ground and various prisoner barracks within the facility. Confederates held here were poorly clothed and ill-fed. Their physical ability to contribute manpower for a serious military effort of a second front is questionable.

Above: The wooden open-bay barracks were very close to the water line and the stockade was no more than a wooden palisade. Had Beall and his party been successful in seizing USS *Michigan*, and had they sufficient expertise to man even some of the guns aboard, the Confederates probably could have overcome the limited Federal defense in the area.

high fence on Johnson's Island. The defenses of the camp were formidable. USS *Michigan*, a vessel in Sandusky Bay, guarded the water approach, while an earth works, Fort Johnson, and the Hoffman Battalion, later part of the 128th Ohio Volunteer Infantry, provided land-side security for the installation. *Michigan* was an iron-hulled steamer about 163 feet long with twelve guns, captained by Commander John C. Carter. Beall intended to seize the ship, the only Federal warship on the Great Lakes, train her guns on the Federal garrison, and force them to release the prisoners. Beall would then use *Michigan* to lay waste to towns on the shores of the Great Lakes, with little fear of opposition, while the released prisoners would run rampant through the interior.

Beall's assault group obtained sufficient small arms, three dozen hatchets and four grappling hooks prior to the raid. On September 19, 1864, Beall and his men began their operation by boarding the steamer *Philo Parsons* in four small groups at four different ports. Beall boarded at Malden, Ontario. The last element had as luggage a large trunk containing all the hatchets, grapnels, rope, revolvers and cutlasses. As the ship approached Middle Bass Island, close to the Ohio shore, Beall and his group drew weapons and clearly identified themselves as Confederate naval

personnel. Shortly after seizing the *Philo Parsons* they approached the *Island Queen*, which was making her regular rounds. Beall's group captured her with a large number of passengers and thirty-two soldiers, all of whom were paroled. Having no use for the second vessel, they sunk her in deep water. Beall and his men on the captured *Philo Parsons* vessel waited anxiously for the other part of the plan to unfold, a signal that the *Michigan* was ready for capture. But nothing happened.

The whole operation hinged on the success or failure of one Rebel soldier, Major Charles H. Cole, 5th Tennessee Cavalry, one of Forrest's officers who had escaped from Johnson's Island in 1863. Cole infiltrated the area days ahead of Beall and his men. Posing as a well-heeled Pennsylvania oil speculator, he cultivated the friendship of the officers of the *Michigan* prior to the planned assault. Cole intended to host a dinner for the naval officers and drug their wine. Then, Cole would fire a rocket to signal successful completion of his part of the mission and Beall and his men would take the *Michigan*. Cole was somehow exposed and arrested by Commander Carter. Without the pre-arranged signal, seventeen of Beall's men lost their nerve and refused to attempt to seize *Michigan*, despite Beall's repeated requests. The mission was aborted.

On September 20 Beall reluctantly sailed *Philo Parsons* to Sandwich, Canada, where they stripped and burned the ship. Federal authorities were able to piece together the whole plan during Cole's subsequent interrogation but, by then, Beall was out of reach.

Beall returned to New York late in the year and was involved in several unsuccessful operations. On his way back to Canada, on December 16, 1864, Beall and George S. Anderson were apprehended near Suspension Bridge, Niagara, and Anderson agreed to become a government witness to avoid prosecution. General John A. Dix, commanding the Department of the East, appointed a Military Commission to try Beall as an insurgent and spy, rather than as a soldier.

The trial began on February 1, 1865, and the outcome was a forgone conclusion. The Confederate officer was allowed little defense, and the fact that he was acting under orders from his military superiors was ignored. Beall was quickly convicted and sentenced to death on February 8. Considerable effort by a number of influential individuals, North and South, was made to have his sentence commuted, to no avail. John Y. Beall was moved to Fort Columbus on Governor's Island and executed there on February 24, 1865. His last words from the scaffold were straightforward: "I protest this execution. It is murder, brutal murder. I die in the defense and service of my country."

One description of his execution is very specific and describes in some detail the peculiar manner in which the sentence was carried out. The device used was on loan from the New York Police Department for the occasion. A chair was placed on a raised scaffold and Beall was seated in the chair with his hands shackled. The rope was placed around his neck but, rather than being dropped through a trap, a counter weight jerked the condemned man up out of the chair in which he was seated, presumably breaking his neck. The coroner's report said he died by strangulation.

Beall was buried February 26 in Greenwood Cemetery in Brooklyn but disinterred at his mother's request on March 22, 1870, and his remains were removed to Zion Episcopal Church in Charles Town, West Virginia.

Michigan, launched in 1842, was the first iron-hulled ship of the U.S. Navy and served until 1905. Renamed *Wolverine,* she was turned over to the Pennsylvania Naval Militia until 1923. All efforts to save her were unsuccessful and the vessel was scrapped in 1949, but her bow and cutwater were saved and are now at the Erie Maritime Museum.

Johnson's Island and the 206 Confederate graves in the cemetery were abandoned by the Federal Government in June 1865. The prison site was farmed sporadically and an attempt to develop the island as a resort in 1897 was a dismal failure. The United Daughters of the Confederacy acquired the cemetery in 1905, erected a monument to the soldiers buried there in 1910, and cared for the site until it was returned to government administration in 1932. The island was declared a National Historic Landmark in 1990.

Left: This monument to more than 200 Confederate dead interred in the small cemetery was all that marked the deserted facility for years. In the last decade considerable interest in the place has been developed and a number of preservation groups are involved.

Below: Fort Johnson was the primary fortification overlooking the Johnson's Island prison compound. The smoothbore barbette guns and one rifle shown here never fired a shot in anger. The government abruptly abandoned the whole installation in June 1865 and allowed it to go to ruin, a victim of postwar downsizing and neglect.

Cushing's Attack on the *Albemarle*

Below left: Lieutenant William Barker Cushing, commanding USS *Monticello* and already a veteran of several special operations, volunteered to lead a night assault to capture or destroy *Albemarle*, then at Plymouth. Secretary of the Navy Gideon Welles described the young naval officer as a "brilliant example of courage and enterprise."

Below right: Commander James W. Cooke, a veteran officer, was captain of the ironclad. He had already seen service aboard CSS *Ellis* on Albemarle Sound, and had been captured and exchanged before he was placed in charge of the completion of *Albemarle*. He became known as the "Ironmonger Captain" for his constant requests to foundries in Richmond and Wilmington for iron to complete the armor of his ship. Cooke almost collapsed from exhaustion and was relieved by Lieutenant Commander Alexander F. Warley.

William Barker Cushing was another of the extraordinary individuals who rose to distinction during the Civil War. Dismissed from the Naval Academy in March 1861, three months prior to graduation, he was appointed an "acting volunteer master's mate" by Secretary of the Navy Gideon Welles. In September 1861 he resigned from service because of a minor misunderstanding with a senior officer, but was again reinstated by the Secretary of the Navy. Whatever his shortcomings, by 1863 Cushing had undertaking several audacious raids, conducted with suicidal bravery, and this had earned him the privilege of communicating at will directly with Welles and Under-Secretary of the Navy Gustavus Vasa Fox, highly unusual for a 20-year-old junior officer. By 1864 Cushing was serving off the North Carolina coast, commanding USS *Monticello*, and had already compiled an unparalleled combat record.

Meanwhile, the deadly armored ram CSS *Albemarle* had led a successful attack on Plymouth and dominated Albemarle Sound, preventing the Federal Navy from ascending the Roanoke River. Typical of his nature, Cushing volunteered to lead a mission against the ram, and Rear Admiral David Dixon Porter promised him promotion to the rank of lieutenant commander if he succeeded.

The target was approximately 158 feet long with a beam of 35 feet and draft of 9 feet. She was powered by two balky steam engines with twin screws generating 200 horsepower, but had a speed of only 5 knots. The 60-foot-long centered casemate, nine feet high, mounted two powerful 6.4-inch Brooke rifles fore and aft on pivot carriages. The fearsome vessel was docked at Plymouth on the Roanoke River, about eight miles up from the Sound. Even with her powerplant shortcomings, the ship had already wreaked devastation against the Union blockading fleet.

Cushing's concept of the mission required special equipment, and the bold raider obtained two picket boats modified to his specifications at the New York Naval Yard in September 1864. These craft were light-draft, single-screw, steam barges about 45 feet long with a beam of 6.5 feet. Each was fitted with a torpedo on a swinging 14-foot boom and a bow-mounted light 12-pounder howitzer. One of the special craft was lost en route to the combat area, but the other successfully made the voyage, and by late fall Cushing was ready.

Master's Mate John Woodman had made several reconnaissances up the Roanoke in early October. He had observed *Albemarle* with engines shut down, moored alongside the wharf, bow downstream, protected by a floating torpedo boom of cypress logs. Cushing put out the word for volunteers and selected his party with special care. Prior to setting off he assembled the assault party and told them: "Not only must you not expect, but you must not hope to return. I can promise you nothing but glory, death or, possibly, promotion. We will have the satisfaction of getting in a good lick at the rebels. That is all."

The group set out in two boats on the evening of October 27, 1864. Cushing and seven sailors manned Picket Boat Number 1. The second boat was crewed by seven other men whose specific task was to man *Albemarle* if she were captured by storm, or to pick up survivors from the primary assault boat if the attack should fail. All were armed with revolvers, cutlasses and hand-grenades. Cushing hoped to overwhelm the skeleton crew aboard

Above: **Federal ships under the command of Lieutenant Commander Francis A. Roe fought** *Albemarle* **on May 5, 1864. USS** *Secaucus, Mattabesett* **and** *Wyalusing,* **heavily armed paddlewheel steamers, supported by four other vessels, confronted** *Albemarle* **and her consorts. After dispersing the smaller Confederate ships the Federal fleet turned on** *Albemarle.* **Roe on** *Secaucus* **tried to ram** *Albemarle* **amidships. The impact destroyed the bow of the wooden Union ship and disabled it. No appreciable damage was done to** *Albemarle,* **which then proceeded to batter all seven Federal ships, winning the day.**

Left: **Cushing's objective was the relatively small but dangerous** *Albemarle,* **a Confederate-designed ironclad that had been built in a cornfield on the Roanoke River, and armed with two pivot-mounted 6.4-inch Brooke rifles firing 100-pound projectiles from a casemate covered by four inches of wrought iron, a very tough customer.**

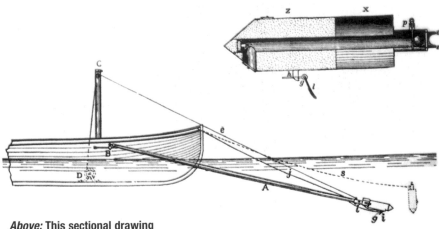

Above: This sectional drawing (top) depicts the explosive charge of the torpedo used by Lieutenant Cushing, and the pulley and boom mechanism used to place the explosive charge under the hull of *Albemarle*, beneath the waterline. The placement of the charge was a very delicate operation, and then the torpedo had to be released from the end of the boom and detonated by pulling a lanyard from the bow of the open boat.

Below: Cushing and crew approached the docked ironclad which was surrounded by a floating log boom. The small steam launch rode up partly over the boom and the torpedo was lowered and exploded. The whole sequence of events took place under the very muzzle of the bow 6.4-inch Brooke rifle, while the little open boat was struck repeatedly by incessant small arms fire from the ironclad and the shore.

the ram and steam her triumphantly down the river out to the U.S. fleet in the Sound.

About a mile below Plymouth the two boats approached the sunken wreck of *Southfield*, a Union sidewheeler steamer that had been mortally hit in a previous attempt to destroy the *Albemarle*. They passed within thirty feet of Confederate pickets stationed on the steamer's still-exposed hurricane deck, without raising any alarm. The river at this point was about 150 yards wide. Sentries around *Albemarle* were more alert and hailed the two boats as they approached. Cushing quickly realized that capture of the ram was not feasible and ordered the second boat to return down river, capture the Confederate picket aboard *Southfield*, and protect his raiding party's line of retreat. Then he ordered his boat full speed ahead.

Lieutenant Alexander F. Warley, commanding *Albemarle*, alerted by the Union reconnaissance of the area, had doubled the guard made up of elements of the 67th North Carolina. The night was dark and rainy but the Federal raiding party was discovered around 3:00 AM on the morning of October

28. The officer of the deck sighted the approaching launch, rang the ship's bell and ordered the deck watch to open fire with small arms. At the same time a bonfire ashore was ignited that illuminated *Albemarle* tied to the wharf and also the torpedo boom surrounding the ram.

Cushing ran his steam launch out into the river so that he could attack in a "bows on" posture. At this point the torpedo was still elevated and not in the water. Small arms fire from *Albemarle* was returned by the little bow-mounted howitzer with a load of canister that clattered off the ironclad's armor plate and cleared the deck as the launch closed on the ironclad. The steam launch struck the torpedo boom but the boat's momentum failed to carry it completely over the obstacle.

Cushing unhesitatingly lowered the spar torpedo into the water against the ram's bow and pulled the lanyard. Bullets ripped through his clothing, buckshot tore off the back of his coat and a bullet tore off the sole of one of his shoes. Cushing was so close he could hear the gun captain aboard the Confederate ironclad shouting orders to the gun crew. The torpedo detonated "abreast of the quarter port." At the same moment the big Brooke rifle fired a charge of grape over the small vessel alongside.

After Cushing's torpedo charge erupted, the *Albemarle* sank at her mooring in a matter of minutes. The blast tore a six-foot hole in the ram's bottom and the wall of water from the explosion doused the little cutter's boiler fire as it bobbed in the water next to the sinking ram. Shipboard Confederates demanded that the Union sailors surrender but Cushing hollered "No!" as *Albemarle* settled in the river.

Cushing shucked off his uniform blouse and shoes, threw away his sword and revolver and told his crew it was every man for himself. Cushing saw fireman Samuel Higgins drown and tried to save Master's Mate Jonathan Woodman, but he also drowned. Ordinary Seaman Edward J. Houghton and Cushing were the only two not killed or captured. Cushing was ultimately the only member of the crew to escape, swimming away and later paddling for ten hours a small boat he found, until he was picked up by the Union vessel *Valley City* close to midnight on September 28/29.

Congress officially thanked Cushing and he became the youngest lieutenant commander in the Federal Navy. By the end of the war he had received four commendations from the Navy Department.

Albemarle was the only Confederate ironclad ram sunk in combat during the war. The vessel was raised on March 20, 1865, and towed to the Norfolk Navy Yard, arriving on April 27, 1865. She was photographed and surveyed by May 18, 1865, and valued at $92,444, with cost of repairs estimated at $21,500. The Washington Prize Court authorized her sale to the U.S. Navy for $79,944, and then the ram was laid up with no need for her service. She floated at a remote wharf in Norfolk for sixteen months while marine life ate into her exposed bottom. The ship was sold for $3,200 at public auction on October 15, 1867, by Messrs. Maupin & Hatton, auctioneers, to J. N. Leonard & Co., and scrapped.

The naval hero experienced severe episodic mental illness in the years after the war. In December 1874 he evidently became violently psychotic and was committed to the Government Hospital for the Insane in Washington, D.C. Cushing died there on December 17, 1874, with his mother and wife at his bedside. He was buried on January 8, 1875, in the cemetery at the Naval Academy at Annapolis. His monument is inscribed "Albemarle" on one side.

A number of artifacts from the historic encounter survive in public museums and repositories. The *Albemarle*'s forward 6.4-inch double-banded Brooke rifle is mounted in front of the Supreme Allied Commander Atlantic (SACLANT) Headquarters at the Norfolk Navy Yard. The ship's bell was taken as a war souvenir by members of the 25th Massachu-

setts Volunteer Infantry and presented by Chaplain Horace James to Post 10, Grand Army of the Republic, in Worcester, Massachusetts. The city museum still has the bell. The Second National flag and logbooks of *Albemarle* are in the collections of the Museum of the Confederacy in Richmond. Other items reside in private collections around the country.

A full-size replica of *Albemarle* may be seen at the Port Columbus Civil War Naval Center in Columbus, Georgia, and the Port O'Plymouth Museum has a floating half-scale replica in their exhibits in North Carolina.

Left: The bow gun could not be depressed enough and luckily fired over the launch, but the force of the torpedo explosion, the concussion from the discharge of the Brooke rifle and the cascading water destroyed the launch. Cushing alone managed to make his way downriver and was picked up by a Federal ship. All the other raiders were captured or drowned. It was a miracle that any of the crew survived.

Below: Cushing said the detonation took place at the same instant of the discharge of the big Brooke gun. The explosion ripped a hole in the hull of the ironclad "big enough to drive a wagon in." *Albemarle* settled quickly to the bottom of the river in eight feet of water, with the upper part of the casemate still exposed.

Forrest's "Cavalry Afloat" Attack on Johnsonville

Below: The earthen redoubt armed with six field guns on the ridge above the Johnsonville Depot was the only defensive position of note when Forrest made his bold raid on the installation. Two other mobile batteries, some scattered rifle pits and picket posts were the only other opposition.

In October 1864 Confederate General Nathan Bedford Forrest's mission was to cut Federal supply lines to Nashville and Atlanta, threaten Paducah, and relieve pressure on the beleaguered Rebel forces. Forrest and Captain John W. Morton, with 3,000 troopers and ten field pieces, left Corinth, Mississippi, on October 19 and rode northwesterly on sore, poorly shod and worn out horses to Jackson, Tennessee, and then northeasterly to Paris Landing. The audacious plan was to blockade the Tennessee River south of the Kentucky state line, and deprive Union General George H. Thomas's troops in Nashville and General William T. Sherman's troops around Atlanta of critically needed supplies.

The primary objective was Johnsonville, a naval station and large depot serving Nashville on the Nashville & Northwestern Railroad. The depot was located twenty-five miles south of Fort Heiman on the Tennessee River, well protected by a fortified garrison under the command of Colonel C. R. Thompson and a fleet of "tinclads" and assorted gunboats under Lieutenant Edward M. King of the United States Navy.

On October 28 Forrest occupied the abandoned Fort Heiman and established a concealed artillery position, a masked battery, south of the fort at Paris Landing. The object was to ambush and capture shipping on the river between the two positions. The Confeder-

ates were successful the next day when they seized *Mazeppa* pulling two barges. The Southerners unloaded her seven hundred tons of cargo of much needed clothing, blankets, shoes, equipment and food and burned the vessel. The steamer *Anna* was badly shot up but managed to escape toward Paducah. Another boat and the *J. W. Cheeseman* were also burned. The Confederates managed to capture intact a transport, *Venus,* and the eight-gun "tinclad" *Undine* (Gunboat No. 55) after a fifty-five minute artillery duel, an unusual accomplishment for cavalry, even Forrest's cavalry! One of Forrest's regimental commanders, Colonel C. R. Barteau, issued an order not found in any manual: "Halt! Dismount and prepare, on foot, to fight gunboats." The events that subsequently occurred have been aptly described as an "inland amphibious maneuver."

Forrest appointed Lieutenant Colonel W. A. Dawson as "commodore" and put him and two twenty-pounder Parrott rifles aboard *Venus.* He then scoured his ranks for former riverboat men to crew the vessel. Captain Frank P. Gracey, a riverboat skipper before the

war, was placed in command of *Undine,* and the battle flag of Forrest's Escort was provided for the vessel. The Southern troopers were transformed into "horse marines" or "cavalry afloat." Brigadier General James Chalmers' division of cavalry and Rice's Battery slogged along the riverbank. Forrest's idea was to have the artillery support the water-borne cavalry in case they encountered Federals on the cruise south. Unfortunately, heavy undergrowth along the bank, rough and hilly roads, and a continuous drizzle slowed their progress.

Escaped crewmen of the captured vessels warned the skeptical Federal officers at Johnsonville of the peculiar assault group heading south. U.S. Navy Lieutenant Edward M. King led gunboats north on November 2 to investigate the strange threat. The Federal *Key West* and *Tawah* came upon *Venus,* way ahead of *Undine* and supporting artillery, as she rounded a bend in the river, and drove her ashore where the Confederates escaped into the woods. The Confederates abandoned the two Parrott rifles on the boat as they escaped, and they were captured by the Federals. Forrest was not amused.

Above left: The installation boasted an extensive rail spur system, sidings, river wharfs and storage facilities. Topography that offered ample opportunity for adequate defensive fortifications was ignored, either because of ignorance or over-confidence. The garrison, commanded by Colonel C. R. Thompson, was ill-prepared to face Forrest's veteran cavalry.

Above: Brigadier General James Ronald Chalmers served well with Forrest in spite of personality conflicts between the two generals over command prerogatives. General Chalmers commanded elements of Forrest's cavalry and artillery that slogged down the almost impassable swamps adjacent to the riverbank to Johnsonville.

Left: Forrest's cavalrymen captured the tinclad *Undine* and turned her eight guns against the Federals ashore and afloat. She was eventually set fire and spectacularly exploded at the riverbank. (Image © Raise the Gunboats, Inc.)

Above: Captain John W. Morton, Forrest's chief of artillery, had four batteries under his command during the raid. His brilliant placement of guns across the river from Johnsonville enabled the Confederates to bring deadly accurate fire on the post and garrison while avoiding counter battery fire from the fort and flotilla.

But the Federals retired rather than engage *Undine* and Morton's artillery lining up on the riverbank. Forrest's soaking wet troopers spent that night huddled in the midst of a massive lightning and thunderstorm that nearly panicked some less seasoned troopers.

The mutually supportive Confederate elements moved further south on the river to Reynoldsburg Island, and established batteries north of the island and south at Pilot Knob to block the river again. Forrest tried to lure the Federal flotilla within range of his artillery, dangling *Undine* alone on the river, but the Federals knew only too well by then with whom they were dealing and refused to take the bait. Meanwhile, young Morton had carefully moved some of his guns on down the river and was quietly sighting them across from the blissfully unaware Federal installation.

On November 3, six Federal gunboats from Paducah attacked *Undine* from the north, up the river, while three others, including their flagship *Key West*, approached *Undine* from the south, down the river. The Confederates on *Undine* and the shore batteries hit the Union flagship nineteen times, but the outnumbered Confederates on the captured ship soon discovered they were out of ammunition for the guns and coal for the boilers. Rather than surrender and be taken prisoner, they ran *Undine* against the bank and fired the vessel, which disintegrated in a spectacular explosion while they escaped into the woods. The victorious Federals nonchalantly returned to Johnsonville, seemingly secure in the belief they had vanquished Forrest.

At 2:00 PM on November 4, John Morton's guns cut loose on Johnsonville at a range of only 500 yards. The artilleryman had chosen his gun positions with such expertise that the Federal garrison, high on a hill, was unable to depress its guns enough to fire on the Confederates along the riverbank, while the guns on the Federal gunboats lacked elevation with which to engage the Rebels. In the excitement of the moment General Forrest enthusiastically helped work one of the guns.

In less than an hour the whole place was in flames, and then direct hits on a large liquor storage area turned the Federal installation into

Right: The supply depot at Johnsonville was the largest in the area and the source of absolutely essential supplies for the armies of George Thomas and William Tecumseh Sherman. The enormous strategic importance of the place to the Union war effort was quickly recognized by General Forrest but seems to somehow have escaped Union commanders in the area.

a roaring inferno. Accounts vary, but the Federals lost at least four, possibly five, gunboats, fourteen steam transports, eighteen to twenty barges, thirty-two or thirty-three pieces of artillery, 75,000 tons of supplies worth around $7,000,000, and the buildings in which they were stored, not to mention 150 prisoners.

The Federal reaction to the disaster was the equivalent of swatting at a fly with a sledgehammer. The entire XXIII Corps arrived the next day and established impregnable defenses around the smoking remains of the depot. But Forrest had already disappeared the previous night, riding off into the darkness lighted by the fires of the burning depot, carrying his two dead and four wounded with him. This was his last independent command and one of the most unusual raids of the war. Forrest earned the accolade "Wizard of the Saddle" many times over by the amazing adaptability and improvisation exhibited in just this type of fluid combat situation.

During the four years of the war Forrest and his command captured thousands of Union troops and seized or destroyed arms, accouterments, other equipment, horses, supplies, even gunboats – in total value that ran into tens of millions of dollars. After the war General Joseph E. Johnston acclaimed Forrest the "the greatest soldier the Civil War produced." General Robert E. Lee said Forrest was the greatest genius to emerge during the war and that "he accomplished more with fewer troops than any other officer on either side." General Sherman probably paid General Forrest his finest compliment when he said he

wanted him hunted down and killed if it cost ten thousand lives and broke the treasury.

The historic area encompassing the Johnsonville raid is mostly under water now, covered by Kentucky Lake, part of the Tennessee Valley Authority. There are ongoing attempts to raise the gunboats, and further information on this can be found on www.gunboats.com.

Below left: The Tennessee River, behind the boxcars, was all that kept the Confederate raiders from overrunning the garrison and capturing Johnsonville intact. The winter camp of part of the garrison is seen to the right and a battery of field artillery without teams stands in front of the loading dock.

Below: The magnificent statue erected in honor of General Nathan Bedford Forrest, considered by many, including his peers, to have been the greatest soldier of the Civil War. The statue stands proudly in Forrest Park, on Union Avenue, a few miles from the center of downtown Memphis.

Read's Dash for the Sea

Charles William Read was the anchorman of the Class of 1860 at the Naval Academy. He graduated dead last and worked hard at it. Required to take French, the only word he mastered was *savez* – "you know." He habitually ended every sentence with that expression and his nickname for the rest of his life was "Savez." The only course in which he excelled was gunnery, taught by Lieutenant John Taylor Wood. Some have said he was not right bright, but no one ever questioned his bravery.

Read resigned from the U.S. Navy on January 19, 1861, the day after he learned that his home state, Mississippi, had seceded. He was appointed an acting midshipman in the Confederate States Navy on April 13, 1861, and ordered to report to CSS *McRae* at New Orleans. By July he had distinguished himself sufficiently to be promoted to acting master and executive officer of *McRae* and assumed command of the ship after the captain was wounded during the Battle of Forts Jackson and St. Philip, April 24, 1862. Read courageously fought *McRae* until she was lost at New Orleans. The Secretary of the Navy wrote, "the conduct of the officers and crew of the *McRae* had rarely been surpassed in the annals of naval warfare." The Confederate Congress subsequently issued a joint resolution thanking Read.

By then he had acquired a reputation for excellence in gunnery, coolness and determination and in June 1862 was assigned with the rank of lieutenant to the heavily armed ironclad CSS *Arkansas* in the Yazoo River. The next month the ironclad ran slowly through the whole Yankee navy, thirty Union vessels, firing all the way, and anchored in front of Vicksburg. In August *Arkansas* went out to fight but

chronic engine failure forced her destruction rather than have her fall into Federal hands.

After a boring stint of shore duty at Port Hudson, Louisiana, Read was assigned to the raider CSS *Florida* at the specific request of Captain John Newland Maffitt for her first cruise, and he was later given independent command of the armed prize brig *Clarence*. The indomitable Read seized and armed the barques *Archer* and *Tacony* and then captured twenty-one other vessels, including the revenue cutter *Caleb Cushing*, armed with a 32-pounder gun. This last ship he actually stole out of the harbor of Portland, Maine, under the guns of Forts Preble, Scammell and Georges and in front of two new gunboats, *Agawam* and *Pontoosuc*. However, the ship was becalmed and Read and his band of raiders were captured.

After nearly a year and a half as a prisoner at Fort Warren in Boston Harbor, where he attempted to escape at every opportunity, Read was exchanged in the fall of 1864 only to be assigned to shore duty in command of Batteries Wood and Semmes on the James River. Boredom set in and he requested permission from Secretary of the Navy Mallory to launch a raid. Emulating his mentor, John Taylor Wood, he proposed to take a small boat on a wagon overland around the Federal flank and launch against the captured ironclad CSS *Atlanta*, which was then anchored in Hampton Roads. Read proposed to sink the ironclad with a torpedo using the proven tactics that had been employed by his old classmate, Lieu-

tenant William B. Cushing, against CSS *Albemarle*. After several frustrating days during which he captured a tug, a barge of forage, a schooner, all of which were destroyed, and thirty prisoners that he didn't need, he returned to Confederate lines, his assault on the *Atlanta* a non-starter.

In early 1865, Read, still spoiling for action, requested assignment to the steam torpedo boats of the *David* class then under construction, but his request was refused. He attempted another "navy on wheels" assault on the twin-turret monitor *Onondaga* at City Point. Unfortunately, the Union ship was already under steam when his small band of raiders arrived and they had to be satisfied with the capture and burning of three schooners laden with forage and a tug. Read wanted to lead yet another amphibious assault against Union shipping at City Point and received permission directly from President Jefferson Davis and General Robert E. Lee. With a mixed all-volunteer army-navy-marine assault team of 120 men, the operation began in early February in freezing rain and ice. After eleven bitterly cold and frustrating days, Read returned from the unsuccessful mission without the loss of a man.

Realizing that the war was winding down, Read wanted one more big adventure. He had heard about the 206-foot sidewheel steamer, CSS *William H. Webb*, still afloat on the Red River in Louisiana. Again, he went to the Secretary of the Navy and requested, just one more time, to be allowed an inde-

Below: Read's last great adventure of the war was his desperate attempt to run CSS *Webb*, a barely floating wreck of a sidewheel steamer, 300 miles through occupied territory, literally under the guns of the Federal Navy, to Cuba. Considering some of his previous adventures, this one was hardly out of character. Cornered below New Orleans, his bag of tricks exhausted, Read ordered *Webb* set fire and destroyed.

pendent "suicide" mission. Read's plan was to load the *Webb* with cotton, go down the Red River to the Atchafalaya River and into the Gulf of Mexico, sail to Cuba, sell the cotton and convert *Webb* to a blockade-runner and steam into Galveston Harbor. Mallory approved the plan on February 17 and even authorized funding for the mission.

Read finally found the *Webb* on March 31, 1865, eighty miles below Shreveport, Louisiana. The former tugboat had been laid up since March 1863, and was barely afloat and falling apart. Read immediately asked for volunteers from local army units and quickly mustered a crew of sixteen officers and fifty-one men. There were no supplies or fuel aboard and the only weapons available were a few cutlasses. Read scrounged a 30-pounder Parrott rifle, two 12-pounder boat howitzers and five 100-pound spar torpedoes for the vessel. His men somehow got the engines running and managed to get the decrepit vessel to Shreveport.

Minimal repairs and modifications were made and the ship was stocked with water and provisions. Read had 190 cotton bales stacked around the engines for protection against enemy fire and was forced to use pine knots for fuel. Finally, he had the steamer whitewashed as an attempt at camouflage. All the additional weight increased the draft of *Webb*

and prohibited use of the Atchafalaya River, so Read was forced to go down the Mississippi River, over 300 miles to the Gulf, all under the control of Federal forces.

On April 16, Read and *Webb* were ready. Rats were seen to scamper off the old boat as she left the wharf, somewhat spooking the crew. At Alexandria, they learned General Lee had already surrendered, and President Lincoln had been assassinated. Nevertheless, Read's sense of honor dictated he continue the mission. *Webb* cast off at 4:30 AM and headed down the Red River for the mighty Mississippi – and a host of Union warships.

Webb faced USS *Lafayette* with 100-pounders, the captured Confederate ironclad, now USS *Tennessee*, with 7-inch Brooke rifles, USS *Gazelle* with only 12-pounders, and the monitor USS *Manhattan* with huge 15-inch Dahlgren guns. Gunboats USS *Vindicator* and USS *Lexington*, as well as steamers USS *Samson* and USS *Champion*, had joined the other Union vessels waiting for *Webb* to appear.

Read calmly ordered full speed ahead and steered for the biggest opening between the Union vessels. The Federals were so flabbergasted that only a few shots were fired at *Webb* as she ran through the anchored Federal ships and disappeared down the dark river. *Webb* shot past the sleeping USS *Hindman* and below

Below: Queen of the West, Tyler and Carondelet engaged CSS Arkansas when she came down the Yazoo River on her run to Vicksburg. During the fight the Captain of Tyler instructed the Captain of the Queen to ram Arkansas but the Queen of the West backed away and ran for safety soon joined by Tyler while Carondelet was disabled. At the time Read commanded the two stern 32-pounder guns of the fearsome ironclad.

the town of Morganza sent a party ashore to cut the telegraph wires. USS *Choctaw* and USS *Hyacinth* were anchored at St. Francisville as *Webb* serenely slid past around 10:00 PM. Next, the Confederates encountered the iron-clad USS *Nymph*, whose crew just watched them pass down river. Telegraph wires were cut again 160 miles above New Orleans.

Read had the ship's lights arranged like those of a Union transport. At Port Hudson, he ordered the *Webb* to slow as they nonchalantly passed in front of the fort's big guns. USS *Naiad* and USS *General Price* again just watched as the disguised Rebels cruised past around 1:30 AM. The Confederates stopped long enough to cut the telegraph wires again. At sunrise the chugging old *Webb* approached Donaldsonville, just seventy-five miles above New Orleans, where the crew cut more wires, and then passed wide-awake USS *Ouachita* as the crew practiced morning gun drill.

Ouachita finally wired New Orleans that *Webb* was running out. Now the whole Union fleet knew Read was coming, but the Federals had no accurate description of the Confederate vessel. Read ordered the *Webb* slowed, the U.S. stars and stripes run up to half-mast because of the president's assassination, the deck gang into blue uniforms and others to lounge about the deck smoking pipes. At high noon *Webb* calmly cruised right through the Union fleet.

The pilot of the USS *Lackawana* finally recognized *Webb* and firing began. A projectile hit the bow of the Confederate ship four feet above the water line and went all the way through the ship and out the other side. Read yelled for full speed ahead and ran up the Confederate flag. Enemy fire wrecked the pilothouse and disabled the bow-mounted spar torpedo. About this time, in the midst of the running firefight, *Webb* passed a visiting French warship and Read had the *sang-froid* to dip the Confederate flag in salute. Then, they were past New Orleans and the whole Union fleet, still afloat. The only recorded casualties were a couple of cows hit by overshoots across the river.

Rumors in New Orleans were mind-boggling. The *Webb* was said to be carrying Jefferson Davis with all the gold and silver of the Confederate treasury with John Wilkes Booth as pilot. The incredible journey continued until they came upon USS *Richmond* fifty miles above Forts Jackson and St. Philip, and Read's luck ran out. The Yankee ship was ready and waiting with her guns run out. Read ordered the *Webb* to be run into the shore and set alight. The old vessel blew up when the flames reached her magazine at 4:30 PM on April 24, 1865.

After futile attempts to escape, Read, mortified at the thought of capture by land forces, returned to the river, hailed a passing ship and surrendered to a Union naval officer, his classmate, Winfield S. Schley. When Read offered his sword to his captor, Schley said, "Hell, Read. Put your sword away and have some coffee."

Read's war was finally over. He was taken back to New Orleans and then confined at Fort Warren again. Charles William Read took the oath of allegiance and was released July 24, 1865. The governor of Louisiana appointed Read president of the Board of Harbor Masters of New Orleans, a position he held until the late 1880s. He died in January 1890 and was buried at Rose Hill Cemetery in Meridian, Mississippi. The small tombstone of the Confederate hero is adorned by a simple fouled anchor.

Below: USS *Indianola*, a 511-ton ironclad gunboat, was run aground and captured on February 24, 1863, by *Webb* and another Confederate vessel. This was the only bright spot in *Webb*'s otherwise uneventful service as a privateer and "cotton clad" ram until "Savez" Read took the vessel through the Union fleet in front of New Orleans on her final run to a rendezvous with history.

Bibliography

Abdill, George B., *Civil War Railroads. Pictorial Story of the Iron Horse, 1861–1865,* New York, Bonanza Books, 1961

Berry, Colonel Thomas F., *Four Years with Morgan and Forrest,* Oklahoma City, OK, The Harlow-Ratliff Company, 1914

Boykin, Edward, *Sea Devil of the Confederacy. The Story of the* Florida *and Her Captain, John Newland Maffitt,* New York, Funk & Wagnalls Co., 1959

Boykin, Edward, *Beefsteak Raid. Wade Hampton and His 1864 Cattle Raid,* New York, Funk & Wagnalls Co., 1960

Brooksher, William R., and Snider, David K., *Glory at a Gallop. Tales of the Confederate Cavalry,* Gretna, Louisiana, Pelican Publishing Company, 2002

Brown, D. Alexander, *Grierson's Raid,* Dayton, OH, Press of Morningside Bookshop, 1981

Campbell, R. Thomas, *Gray Thunder, Exploits of the Confederate States Navy,* Shippensburg, PA, The Burd Street Press, 1996

Carter, Arthur B., *The Tarnished Cavalier, Major General Earl Van Dorn, C.S.A.,* Knoxville, University of Tennessee Press, 1999

Cullen, Joseph P., *The Peninsula Campaign, 1862,* Harrisburg, PA, The Stackpole Company, 1973

Current, Robert N., Editor-in-Chief, *Encyclopedia of the Confederacy,* 4 volumes, New York and London, Simon & Schuster, Inc. 1993

Daughtry, Mary Bandy, *Gray Cavalier. The Life and Wars of General W. H. F. "Rooney" Lee,* Cambridge, MA, Da Capo Press, 2002

Davis, Burke, *Jeb Stuart. The Last Cavalier,* New York, Rinehart & Company, Inc. 1957

deKay, James Tertius, *The Rebel Raiders. The Astonishing History of the Confederacy's Secret Navy,* New York, Ballantine Books, 2002

Elliott, Robert G., *Ironclad of the Roanoke. Gilbert Elliott's Albemarle,* Shippensburg, PA, White Mane Publishing Company, 1994

Faust, Patricia I., Editor, *Historical Times Illustrated Encyclopedia of the Civil War,* New York, Harper & Row, Publishers, 1986

Gilder, R. W., Editor-in-Chief, *Battles and Leaders of the Civil War,* 4 volumes, New York, The Century Company, 1887

Hinds, John W., *The Hunt for the Albemarle. Anatomy of a Gunboat War,* Shippensburg, PA, Burd Street Press, 2001

Hoole, William Stanley, *Four Years in the Confederate Navy. The Career of Captain John Low on the CSS* Fingal, Florida, Alabama, Tuscaloosa *and* Ajax, Athens, GA, University of Georgia Press, 1964

Horan, James D., editor, *CSS* Shenandoah. *The Memoirs of Lieutenant Commanding James I. Waddell,* New York, Crown Publishers, Inc., 1960

Hudgins, Garland C., and Kleese, Richard B., editors, *Recollections of an Old Dominion Dragoon, The Civil War Experiences of Sgt. Robert S. Hudgins, II, Co. B, 3rd Virginia Cavalry,* Orange, VA, Publisher's Press, Inc., 1993

Hurst, Jack, *Nathan Bedford Forrest,* New York, Alfred A. Knopf, 1993

Longacre, Edward G., *Mounted Raids of the Civil War,* Lincoln, NE, and London, University of Nebraska Press, 1975

Longacre, Edward G., *Lee's Cavalrymen. A History of the Mounted Forces of the Army of Northern Virginia.* Mechanicsburg, PA, Stackpole Books, 2002

Longacre, Edward G., *Gentleman and Soldier. A Biography of Wade Hampton, III,* Nashville, The Rutledge Hill Press, 2003

Headley, John W., *Confederate Operations in Canada and New York,* Alexandria, VA, Time-Life Collector's Library of the Civil War, 1981

Hearn, Chester G., *Naval Battles of the Civil War,* San Diego, CA, Advantage Publishers Group, 2000

Herr, John K., and Wallace, Edward S., *The Story of the U.S. Cavalry, 1775–1942,* New York, Bonanza Books, 1984

Johnson, Clint, *Civil War Blunders,* Winston-Salem, NC, John F. Bair, Publisher, 1997

Jones, J., William, Rev. D. D, *Southern Historical Society Papers,* 52 volumes, Millwood, NJ, Krauss Reprint, 1977

Jones, Virgil Carrington, *Gray Ghosts and Rebel Raiders. The Daring Exploits of the Confederate Guerrillas,* New York, Promontory Press, 1995

Lytle, Andrew Nelson, *Bedford Forrest and His Critter Company,* New York, G. P. Putman's Sons, 1931

McAulay, John D., *Carbines of the Civil War, 1861–1865,* Union City, TN, Pioneer Press, 1981

McAulay, John D., *Civil War Carbines. Volume II, The Early Years,* Lincoln, RI, Andrew Mowbray Inc. Publishers, 1991

Martin, Samuel J., *"Kill-Cavalry". The Life of General Hugh Judson Kilpatrick,* Rutherford, NJ, Fairleigh Dickinson University Press, 1996

Maness, Lonnie E., *An Untutored Genius. The Military Career of General Nathan Bedford Forrest,* Oxford, MS, The Guild Bindery Press, 1990

Miller, Francis Trevelyan, Editor-in-Chief, *The Photographic History of the Civil War,* 10 Volumes, New York, The Review of Reviews Co., 1911

Moseley, Cameron, *John Yates Beall. Confederate Commando,* Great Falls, VA, Clan Bell International, 2001

O'Neill, Charles, *Wild Train. The Story of the Andrews Raiders,* New York, Random House, 1956

Owsley, Frank Lawrence, Jr., *The C.S.S. Florida. Her Building and Operation,* Tuscaloosa, AL, and London, The University of Alabama Press, 1965

Petersen, Paul R., *Quantrill of Missouri. The Making of a Guerrilla Warrior,* Nashville, TN, Cumberland House, 2003

Pittenger, William, *The Great Locomotive Chase. A History of the Andrews Railroad Raid into Georgia in 1862,* Philadelphia, The Penn Publishing Company, 1908

Roberts, W. Adolphe, *Semmes of the Alabama,* Indianapolis and New York, The Bobbs-Merrill Company, 1938

Scharf, J. Thomas, *History of the Confederate States Navy from its Organization to the Surrender of its Last Vessel,* 1887, reprinted New York, The Fairfax Press, 1977

Schneller, Robert J., Jr., *Cushing. Civil War SEAL,* Washington, D.C., Brassey's Inc., 2004

Soley, James Russell, *The Blockade and The Cruisers,* Wilmington, NC, Broadfoot Publishing Company, 1989

Shingleton, Royce Gordon, *John Taylor Wood. Sea Ghost of the Confederacy,* Athens, GA, The University of Georgia Press, 1979

Starr, Stephen Z., *The Union Cavalry in the Civil War,* 3 volumes, Baton Rouge, Louisiana State University Press, 1979–85

Still, William N., Jr., Taylor, John M., and Delaney, Norman C., *Raiders and Blockaders. The American Civil War Afloat,* Washington and London, Brassey's, 1998

Thomason, John W., Jr., *JEB Stuart,* New York and London, Charles Scribner's Sons, 1930

Williamson, James J., *Mosby's Raiders,* Alexandria, VA, Time-Life Collector's Library of the Civil War, 1982

Warner, Ezra J., *Generals in Blue. Lives of the Union Commanders,* Baton Rouge, Louisiana State University Press, 1981

Warner, Ezra J., *Generals in Gray. Lives of the Confederate Commanders,* Baton Rouge, Louisiana State University Press, 1978

Wills, Brian Steel, *A Battle from the Start. The Life of Nathan Bedford Forrest,* New York, HarperCollins Publishers, 1993

Wyeth, John A., *Life of General Nathan Bedford Forrest,* New York and London, Harper & Brothers Publishers, 1908

Picture Credits

In addition to the images supplied by people and organizations referred to in the acknowledgments, many other photographs were provided by Russ A. Pritchard, Jr, and Ray Bonds, from the Library of Congress, National Archives, the U. S. Navy Museum and History Center, and also as follows: pages 18 (bottom right), 20 (top and bottom), 21 (top), 22, The Southern Museum of Civil War and Locomotive History, Kennesaw. Every effort has been made to trace and contact the sources of images used in this book; the publishers apologize to owners or copyright holders if any image has been reproduced without credit.

Index